TRAVEL + LEISURE

UNEXPECTEDUSA

A pair of lift operators at Buttermilk, in Aspen, Colorado. Photographed by Martha Camarillo.

TRAVEL + LEISURE

UNEXPECTEDUSA

TRAVEL
+LEISURE
BOOKS

AMERICAN EXPRESS PUBLISHING CORPORATION
NEW YORK

4

EDITOR Irene Edwards
CONSULTING EDITOR Laura Begley
ART DIRECTOR Wendy Scofield
ASSOCIATE MANAGING EDITOR Laura Teusink
ASSISTANT BOOK EDITOR James Jung
PHOTO EDITOR Beth Garrabrant
REPORTERS Lisa Cheng, Sarah Khan, Kathryn O'Shea-Evans
COPY EDITORS David Gunderson, Diego Hadis, Sarah Khan, Elizabeth Sentz
RESEARCHERS Peter Fox, Shira Nanus, Paola Singer
PRODUCTION ASSOCIATE David Richey

TRAVEL + LEISURE

EDITOR-IN-CHIEF Nancy Novogrod
CREATIVE DIRECTOR Bernard Scharf
EXECUTIVE EDITOR Jennifer Barr
MANAGING EDITOR Mike Fazioli
ARTS/RESEARCH EDITOR Mario R. Mercado
SENIOR COPY EDITOR Kathy Roberson
PRODUCTION DIRECTOR Rosalie Abatemarco-Samat
PRODUCTION MANAGER Ayad Sinawi

AMERICAN EXPRESS PUBLISHING CORPORATION

PRESIDENT AND CHIEF EXECUTIVE OFFICER Ed Kelly
CHIEF MARKETING OFFICER AND PRESIDENT, DIGITAL MEDIA Mark V. Stanich
CHIEF FINANCIAL OFFICER AND SENIOR VICE PRESIDENT, CORPORATE DEVELOPMENT AND OPERATIONS Paul B. Francis
VICE PRESIDENTS, GENERAL MANAGERS Keith Strohmeier, Frank Bland
VICE PRESIDENT, BOOKS AND PRODUCTS, AND PUBLISHER Marshall Corey
DIRECTOR, BOOK PROGRAMS Bruce Spanier
SENIOR MARKETING MANAGER, BRANDED BOOKS Eric Lucie
ASSISTANT MARKETING MANAGER Lizabeth Clark
DIRECTOR OF FULFILLMENT AND PREMIUM VALUE Phil Black
MANAGER OF CUSTOMER EXPERIENCE AND PRODUCT DEVELOPMENT Charles Graver
DIRECTOR OF FINANCE Tom Noonan
ASSOCIATE BUSINESS MANAGER Uma Mahabir
OPERATIONS DIRECTOR Anthony White

Front cover: A dockside lobster shack on Cape Porpoise, Maine.
Photographed by Hugh Stewart

ISBN 978-0-7566-7210-2

Published by American Express Publishing Corporation
1120 Avenue of the Americas
New York, New York 10036

Distributed by DK Publishing, Inc.
375 Hudson Street, New York, New York 10014

Manufactured in China

On Zuma Beach, in Malibu, California, near Los Angeles. Photographed by Jessica Schwartzberg.

Vinyl records at John Varvatos Bowery, in New York City. Photographed by Andrea Fazzari.

CONTENTS

An outrigger canoe on Waikiki
Beach near the Royal Hawaiian
hotel, in Oahu. Photographed
by Jessica Schwartzberg.

INTRODUCTION

BY NANCY NOVOGROD, Editor-in-Chief, *Travel + Leisure*

To some people, covering destinations within the United States might seem like an easy way to fill the pages of a New York–based travel magazine. For the most part, the places are reasonably accessible, there's a common language, and, at least at heart, there's a common culture. But who would deny the profusion of topographical, geographical, social, and political differences that separate each state, city, town, and hamlet from its neighbor— sometimes even conferring a surprising foreignness on the spot next door?

In celebration of this rich diversity, we present *Unexpected USA*—the third in *Travel + Leisure*'s book series, following on the heels of *Unexpected France* and *Unexpected Italy*. In some ways this volume, bringing together 16 of our favorite articles on American destinations, may well be the most unexpected of all. From Alaska to Florida, city to beach, each story comes with surprising new twists. For instance, did you know that one of America's most exciting wine regions is rural, unassuming Walla Walla, in Washington State? Or that the Midwest is a treasure trove of buildings by some of the world's leading architects? Or that the celebrity-studded ski town of Aspen, Colorado, harbors a countercultural soul? To be sure, you'll also find reassuringly familiar types: wranglers at a rustic-chic ranch in Montana, lobstermen at shacks in coastal Maine, and surfers at a laid-back seaside retreat on Florida's Gulf Coast.

Included with each story is a guide that will help you uncover the best of the region—hotels, restaurants, sights, and more. Vivid photographs depict a seemingly endless supply of local bounty, from pristine oysters in northern California to smoked ribs in Kansas City. And speaking of bounty, *Unexpected USA* also chronicles our nation's vital arts and culture scene, in the quirky enclaves of downtown Los Angeles; the galleries of the 21c Museum Hotel, in Louisville, Kentucky; the flashy glass towers of the CityCenter complex, on the Las Vegas Strip; and the tiny town of Marfa, a modern art pilgrimage site in the middle of the west Texas desert.

After all, what could be more American than hitting the road and venturing out to discover a new and welcoming place? Wishing you safe and fulfilling journeys—you've got miles and miles to go.

Amoeba Music, in Los Angeles.

A pool at Aspen Meadows Resort.

A beer from DBGB Kitchen & Bar, in Downtown New York.

A staff cabin at Camp Denali, Alaska.

DESTINATIONS

NEW YORK DOWNTOWN

Photographed by Andrea Fazzari

IS IT A PLACE OR A STATE OF MIND? AS MANHATTAN'S HISTORIC BOHEMIAN CENTER UNDERGOES ITS LATEST TRANSFORMATION, WE TAKE A LOOK AT THE BIG IDEAS, CUTTING-EDGE ARCHITECTURE, AND DARING PERSONALITIES THAT ARE SHAPING THE *NEW* NEW YORK. BY PETER JON LINDBERG

NO ONE CAN AGREE ON PRECISELY WHEN IT STARTED, LET ALONE WHERE IT STARTS.

South of Houston Street? 14th? 23rd? Does it include the farther-flung galleries of Chelsea? The Financial District? Do the leafier blocks of the West Village still count, or are check-cashing joints and graffiti a prerequisite? Some say Downtown New York is less a place than an idea, more about sensibility than geography. (For the purposes of our discussion, let's call it the swath between 14th and Chambers Streets, from the Hudson to the East River.)

The one thing New Yorkers can agree on is that Downtown just *feels* different. You sense it the minute you cross that disputed border. Few cityscapes have such recognizable iconography—the cast-iron façades of SoHo, the Belgian block–paved lanes of TriBeCa, the water towers punctuating rooflines like squat wooden rocket ships, the hoardings plastered with dance-mix ads, the congee joints and Puerto Rican bodegas, the bodega that last Tuesday became a bistro.

Funky. Gritty. Hip. Eccentric. Indie. Irreverent. Cool. The prefix *Downtown* has come to connote all sorts of things, not all of them endemic to Lower Manhattan. Downtown's attitude and aesthetic have been codified, commodified, and sold in a million pieces, such that any clued-in kid visiting from the mainland can dress the part and pass as a local. And while it's still the de facto hub, Downtown no longer corners the countercultural market in New York. Artists, designers, and musicians—and the galleries, shops, and clubs that support them—are increasingly drawn to the cheaper reaches of way-Uptown and the outer boroughs. It's a sign of the times that most of New York's top rock acts (MGMT; TV on the Radio; the National; the Yeah Yeah Yeahs; Santigold; the Hold Steady) are based in Brooklyn.

You might conclude that the bohemian culture Downtown nurtured as its own has up and moved elsewhere. No question, this isn't the Lower Manhattan of your uncle's hard-core band. Money, both corporate and private, plays more of a role here than ever: the median price of a two-bedroom condo is about $1.4 million, compared with $315,000 in 1993. Not even 9/11 could knock Downtown off its gentrifying trajectory. Today, the area has far fewer art galleries, far fewer poetry clubs, and six American Apparel stores. It

OPPOSITE: The New Museum, on the Bowery, with Swiss artist Ugo Rondinone's *Hell, Yes!* installation. PREVIOUS SPREAD: Lower Manhattan at dusk, as seen from the New Museum.

is markedly easier to buy eye shadow than a New York Dolls record.

Yet underneath the spit-shine gloss—in the cracks between La Perla and L'Occitane—that churning, inventive, pioneering spirit improbably surges on. You can see it in the young provocateurs of fashion, art, and design who followed their muse to Lower Manhattan, in spite of the costs. You can hear it at experimental music venues like (Le) Poisson Rouge and the Stone (run by avant-garde hero and longtime Downtowner John Zorn). You can knock it back in the innovative breed of cocktail bars—including PDT, Pegu Club, Mayahuel, and Death & Co.—that are transforming New York nightlife. Downtown has

become the anchor of the city's restaurant scene, as well as the preferred location for new hotels. And after decades in the doldrums, New York is finally back to creating bold architecture, much of it below 14th Street: Witness the fabulous New Museum, opened in 2007 on the Bowery, and, nearby, the soon-to-rise headquarters for the Sperone Westwater gallery, designed by Norman Foster. Even those interloping luxury brands and national chains are copping a Downtown edge: consider Derek Lam's striking SoHo store, by Japanese firm SANAA (who also designed the New Museum), or J.Crew's actually-quite-hip men's emporium in TriBeCa, the Liquor Store (co-conceived by Andy Spade).

"If one reads anything about the history of New York, one sees that it's a whole different city every ten years," says Sean MacPherson, who, with his Bowery Hotel, has done plenty to define the current phase. I'd say his timetable is off by about, oh, 10 years. These days, Downtown changes itself every other week.

MORE THAN MOST PARTS OF NEW YORK, Downtown readily evokes Then and Now, Before and After. History is forever bursting to the surface here, like the underlayers of subway posters for last season's blockbusters. For this reason Downtown also evokes in its denizens a keen sense of nostalgia, usually of the pessimistic sort: "Everything went downhill after Florent/CBGB/the Mudd Club closed. Alphabet City was better when it was just artists and dealers and thieves. TriBeCa was better when it didn't exist." I moved to Manhattan at age 24—in time to catch Jeff Buckley at Sin-é but too late to glimpse Jean-Michel Basquiat chalk-painting sidewalks. Whenever you arrived, it seems, you were either too late or too old.

A favorite lament concerns the Fall of SoHo— where, eight years ago, in a metaphor too preposterous to make up, the Downtown branch of the Guggenheim Museum was replaced by a Prada store. It's true that SoHo's most recent metamorphosis is startling even in a city defined by metamorphoses. But too often we neglect the long view—and across its history, the curious expanse between Houston and Canal Streets has seen plenty of ebbs and flows. Mostly farmland in the 18th century, it became, by 1825, one of the richest and most densely populated neighborhoods in Manhattan. John Jacob Astor was a principal landowner. But trendiness had its drawbacks. The 1860's saw an influx of high-end retail—Tiffany; Lord & Taylor—that forced out a quarter of its residents. (Does any of this sound familiar?) It was at this time that SoHo's iconic architecture took shape: the grandly ornamented commercial buildings and warehouses clad in cast iron. But in the 1890's retailers began relocating uptown, and SoHo spiraled into decline; through the first half of the 20th century it became a wasteland known as Hell's Hundred Acres.

"The Fluxus artist George Maciunas really pioneered SoHo as a place to live and work," explains Lisa Phillips, director of SoHo's New Museum. Starting on Wooster Street in 1967, Maciunas set up co-ops in disused cast-iron

DOWNTOWN IS A PLACE OF ENDLESS COLLISIONS AND NEAR-MISSES, WHERE DISPARATE WORLDS RUB UP AGAINST ONE ANOTHER WITH FAMILIARITY

buildings. So began the rise of New York's most famous artists' colony. "It was about more than just affordable space," Phillips says. "It was about seeing beauty in unconventional environments—living in those interzones, in places that people wouldn't normally think of as appropriate or safe."

It's easy to forget how desolate the city used to feel south of Houston Street. In 1970, TriBeCa had only 243 residents. Today, it has 26,151. Downtown still came off as a wild, vaguely menacing frontier as late as 1985, when Martin Scorsese shot his cult classic *After Hours* here. The film starred Griffin Dunne as an Uptown Mr. Jones lost down the rabbit hole of pre–hedge fund SoHo and TriBeCa. In the course of one long night he's accosted by burglars and mohawked punks, flummoxed by a kinky sculptress, chased by an angry mob, and ultimately sent back to Midtown encased in plaster of paris.

"At the time it was all just called Downtown," Dunne recalls. "Terms like NoHo, TriBeCa, and Nolita hadn't taken form yet. And it was truly a no-man's-land. There was no traffic to block—we would shoot all night long and no one would bother us."

You certainly couldn't find a place to spend the night back then, unless you count three-dollar SRO's. High-end hotels were scarce Downtown until the mid-90's, when a handful of boutique properties made inroads. Now they're on every other block. The past two years have ushered in Robert De Niro's Greenwich Hotel, in TriBeCa; Sean MacPherson's cheap-chic Jane Hotel, in the

OPPOSITE: New York- and Vancouver-based band the Albertans at (Le) Poisson Rouge nightclub, on Bleecker Street.

West Village; André Balazs's the Standard, New York; the Cooper Square Hotel, designed by Carlos Zapata Studio; and the recently opened Crosby Street Hotel, in SoHo, the first stateside property from London's ever-stylish Firmdale group.

Downtown's hotel boom has helped to lure a relatively new demographic over the past decade: tourists. Indeed, some weekends there appear to be more visitors on Spring Street than in Times Square. No surprise, either, for SoHo and its satellite neighborhoods have become retail destinations to rival Madison Avenue, with both global and homegrown brands, outsize designer flagships and back-alley boutiques cheek-by-jowl.

Today even Uptown girls stray as far south as (gasp!) Howard Street, on the grungy fringes of Chinatown, to peruse the racks at Opening Ceremony. Carol Lim and Humberto Leon—U.C. Berkeley grads who'd worked for Bally and Burberry—cofounded the boutique in 2002, selling their own line of clothing alongside a mix of labels from Europe, Asia, and South America. A branch in Los Angeles followed. In August the duo opened an eight-story department store in Tokyo. But their hearts remain in Lower Manhattan, specifically the "alternate universe" of Howard Street.

"This is a tiny pocket of Old New York," Lim tells me. "Even when we opened, it was deserted after seven p.m." Yet they found plenty of kindred spirits. "Up the block is E. Vogel, the 120-year-old custom shoe place; Ted Muehling, who's made jewelry around here since the nineties; and newer stores like De Vera and BDDW—it's this incredible little street."

THE CULINARY LANDSCAPE, TOO, HAS exploded. In contrast to a decade ago, most of New York's restaurants-of-the-moment—those that aren't in Brooklyn—are below 14th Street: the Spotted Pig, Locanda Verde, the Waverly Inn & Garden, and the genre-defying, destination-defining restaurants of Keith McNally (including Balthazar, in SoHo; Pastis, in the Meatpacking District; Schiller's Liquor Bar, on the Lower East Side; and the new Minetta Tavern, in Greenwich Village). And then there are the Lower East Side's WD-50, where relentlessly innovative Wylie Dufresne conjures his metaphysical cuisine, and David Chang's border-jumping Momofuku empire in the East Village. It's hard to imagine these latter restaurants—defiantly casual, offbeat, often quite affordable—existing anywhere but Downtown. And its appeal—for both diners and restaurateurs—remains undiminished (if not enhanced) by the area's gentrification. As Graydon Carter, co-owner of the Waverly Inn, says, "In any other city, *downtown* connotes a raffish, unbathed, countercultural sensibility—what Republicans would call 'edgy.' In New York it's all of that, plus it's geographically accurate."

Even Uptown chefs are migrating south. Daniel Boulud, whose namesake French restaurant sets the standard for Upper East Side fine dining, has arrived on the Bowery, of all places, with a resolutely informal, resoundingly loud boîte called DBGB Kitchen & Bar. (Yes, the name is a pun on CBGB, whose former quarters are just up the block; the legendary rock club closed in 2006.) Hearing the Replacements blasting while sampling Boulud's note-perfect charcuterie is quite the novelty. But if there's a disconnect between his name and the neighborhood, Boulud doesn't see it. "I've been a New Yorker for twenty-five years, and just happened to drop my suitcase Uptown," he says. "I've been coming down here just as long—partying, visiting friends. So opening a restaurant here seemed natural."

But Boulud might not have chosen this quirky strip were it not for the futuristic edifice looming down the street. The New Museum recalls a seven-story stack of gift boxes (an allusion to SoHo's retail transformation?). The setting is incongruous: two blocks north of a shop with a sign proffering CASH REGISTERS, SLICERS, SCALES, BANDSAWS and two doors up from the Bowery Mission homeless shelter. Yet the museum embraces its context with an exuberant HELL, YES! (so reads the rainbow-colored sign on the façade, an installation by Swiss artist Ugo Rondinone). The purview is global, yet the curators are dedicated to exhibiting artists who still live and work in Downtown, such as the up-and-coming Corsican-born multimedia artist Agathe Snow and established names like Laurie Simmons.

Artist and 35-year Downtown resident Laurie Simmons inside the New Museum, above left. RIGHT: The rock-and-roll-inspired John Varvatos store on the Bowery, which occupies the former space of the iconic CBGB club.

"We were keen to bring a great work of architecture to the city, and to this street specifically," Phillips says. "The hope is that the Bowery will become a sort of laboratory for experimentation in architecture and design." It's certainly become a bona-fide tourist destination. And the museum has spurred an unexpected revival of the Bowery: besides DBGB and the Bowery Hotel, recent openings include Double Crown, a restaurant-lounge from design collective AvroKO; the clothing emporium Blue & Cream; Bowery Electric, a bar and rock club co-owned by musician Jesse Malin; a new pizzeria from McNally; and, in the former CBGB space, a splashy John Varvatos store.

Hold on, you say—the birthplace of punk rock is now a fashion boutique? Well, as Dave Navarro of Jane's Addiction put it recently, "Better this than a Pinkberry." To Varvatos's credit, rock and roll has always been part of his brand's aesthetic; he even hosts a monthly music show on Sirius XM. The Detroit native vividly

recalls his first trip to New York in 1977—a pilgrimage to see the Ramones at CBGB. Now, in CB's old digs, Varvatos embraces his inner rock geek: selling vintage vinyl, displaying punk memorabilia, staging free concerts, and treating the room less like a clothing store than, well, a club. "We see it as a cultural space," he says. "No way are we trying to emulate what was here before, but we wanted to keep to the history, and to keep music alive in the Bowery. We have a stage and a P.A., so on any given day, people show up and play—the guys from Cheap Trick, Ringo Starr, the New York Dolls." And plenty of curious young rock fans who aren't remotely interested in fashion drop in to the store just to see where CBGB once was.

DOWNTOWN NEW YORK IS A PLACE OF ENDLESS collisions and near-misses, where disparate worlds rub up against one another with remarkable familiarity. Here's Yonah Schimmel's bakery (opened in 1910) abutting an art-house cinema;

there's the Bowery Hotel sidling up to a methadone clinic. In an East Village basement, the sultry speakeasy PDT hides behind an unmarked door in a hot dog joint, while over on the West Side, a derelict elevated freight railroad is abloom with flowers, transformed into the city's newest park.

The High Line—the former railroad in question—is an apt symbol for Downtown's quirky charms, struggles, and (continual) rebirth. Yet were it not for the vision of two ordinary citizens, artist Robert Hammond and writer Joshua David, the High Line might be just a memory. Hammond moved to New York in 1993 and was captivated by the Meatpacking District and West Chelsea—semi-industrial areas "that weren't traditionally beautiful, that some consider eyesores." The High Line in particular caught his imagination: a rusted jumble of steel girders, concrete, and shadow that wound through Manhattan's far west side. Built in the 1930's, the 1.45-mile-long railway had been unused since

1980 and was marked for demolition. At a community board hearing on the subject in 1999, Hammond met David, and the two founded Friends of the High Line, an advocacy group dedicated to saving the structure. FHL would go on to raise $150 million to recast the railway as a pedestrian park.

"Downtown has more of the juxtapositions I love about New York—the glamorous and the gritty, the hard and the soft, the old and the new," Hammond says. "That's why I love the High Line: Who would have imagined a steel structure with wildflowers growing on top?" The first section of the park opened in spring 2009 to rave reviews.

"IT'S SPECIFICALLY A DOWNTOWN THING. IT could go anywhere, but it makes more sense here." Andy Spade—founder of Jack Spade, husband of Kate, and all-around Renaissance man—is discussing his latest venture, Partners & Spade, an ephemera shop/exhibition space/creative

The eclectic inventory of Partners & Spade, in NoHo, above left. RIGHT: High Line advocates and community activists Robert Hammond *(left)* and Joshua David at the park they helped create, set in a defunct railbed.

consultancy headquartered on Great Jones Street. On any given day P&S's stock might include riding crops, antique globes, Super Balls, and a vintage photography book titled *Brokers with Hands on Their Faces*. For a time they also sold vintage guns. Oh, and live birds.

Spade remains dedicated to Downtown, but he admits misgivings. "It doesn't have as much diversity as it did, just because of how expensive it is to live and rent space here. I think half of Downtown has moved to Brooklyn," he says.

There are those who feel Downtown has betrayed itself—or, more to the point, them— in the name of mammon, that money has broken Downtown's spirit. Resentment over gentrification is nothing new, but it's grown increasingly bitter in the past 15 years. (That Guggenheim-Prada switch didn't help.) "For the first time in Manhattan's history, it has no

RUSS & DAUGHTERS IS THE SORT OF SPOT WHERE YOU MIGHT JOIN A NONAGENARIAN WIDOW, A TATTOOED DRUMMER, AND HARVEY KEITEL IN LINE

bohemian frontier," declared Adam Gopnik in *The New Yorker* in 2007. "Another bookstore closes, another theater becomes a condo, another soulful place becomes a sealed residence." MacPherson seconds Gopnik's alarm: "I often wonder, *Do we really need so many banks?*"

But if the effects of millennial prosperity were undeniable, the effects of recession are now plainly visible. Storefront vacancy rates in New York are at their highest since the early 1990's, and a full one in 10 retail spaces in SoHo were recently unoccupied. "With prices loosening up a little," MacPherson says, "there might be more room for more adventurous projects."

So will the softening of the real estate market spark a revival? Will poets and sculptors recolonize Lower Manhattan? Phillips is optimistic. "Downtown still represents the vanguard of the counterculture. There's still a lot of renegade thinking that takes place here—and the downturn is going to bring even more changes."

OPPOSITE: Russ & Daughters, a 90-year-old, family-owned Lower East Side landmark.

"Art and music do seem to be more inspired when people are struggling," Jesse Malin observes. "Downtown always needs that next kick in the ass."

IF NOVELTY IS ONE OF THE ONLY CONSTANTS in New York, there are also places whose constancy is the novelty. Places that have held on so long they might as well be preserved in vinegar. Places like Russ & Daughters, the Jewish "appetizing" shop that's occupied the same Houston Street storefront since 1920. It's the sort of spot where you might join a nonagenarian widow, a tattooed drummer, and Harvey Keitel in line for bagels and whitefish.

"All these hipsters who've settled in the neighborhood are now discovering us," says Niki Russ Federman, the 32-year-old great-granddaughter of founder Joel Russ. "You'll see them chatting with the grandmothers, sharing tips—'Oh, you have to try the wasabi-roe and cream-cheese sandwich!'"

Federman remembers a wholly different neighborhood from her youth, when the Lower East Side was still dominated by working-class families. Its transformation into a trendsetters' bastion is now complete, though traces of the Old World remain: in the cacophonous weekend marketplace on Orchard Street; in the discount underwear shops run by Orthodox Jews; in the brilliantly conceived Lower East Side Tenement Museum, which documents the era when this immigrants' ghetto was the densest conurbation on earth.

Federman studied for an MBA at Yale and worked in international development and health care and as a yoga teacher until a few years ago, when she began to consider joining the family business. She got an unexpected boost from a Downtown icon. "I was at a friend's party, and Lou Reed happened to be there," she recalls. "I'd brought some hors d'oeuvres from Russ & Daughters, and Lou was hovering around the table, devouring the smoked salmon. Someone finally told him who I was. He marched right over and shook my hand and said 'Niki, I just wanted to say—you're New York royalty.' Lou Reed! I almost dropped on the floor." And when Lou Reed speaks, Downtowners listen. Not long afterward she started work at the shop.

14th St.

Fifth Ave.

Broadway

Houston St.

Delancey St.

Canal St.

Chambers St.

Broadway

East River

The Standard, New York.

WHERE TO EAT + DRINK

7. Corton Modern French cuisine in a minimalist setting. *239 W. Broadway; 212/219-2777; dinner for two* ✗✗✗✗.

8. DBGB Kitchen & Bar Chef Daniel Boulud's first downtown venture. *299 Bowery; 212/933-5300; dinner for two* ✗✗✗.

9. Double Crown Cocktails and cuisine inspired by the British empire. *316 Bowery; 212/254-0350; dinner for two* ✗✗✗.

10. L'Artusi Boldly flavored Italian food and a lively, convivial atmosphere. *228 W. 10th St.; 212/255-5757; dinner for two* ✗✗✗.

11. Locanda Verde Robert De Niro's latest TriBeCa trattoria, housed in the Greenwich Hotel. *377 Greenwich St.; 212/925-3797; dinner for two* ✗✗✗.

DBGB Kitchen & Bar.

3. Crosby Street Hotel
Quirky-yet-posh touches of modern London. *79 Crosby St.; 212/226-6400; crosbystreethotel. com; doubles from $$.*

4. Greenwich Hotel In the heart of TriBeCa, with the city's most serene pool. *377 Greenwich St.; 877/888-1255; thegreenwich hotel.com; doubles from $$.*

5. Jane Hotel Affordable railroad car–style rooms and a cozy wood-paneled bar. *113 Jane St.; 212/924-6700; thejanenyc.com; doubles from $.*

6. Standard, New York
Impossibly hip glass hotel presiding over the Meatpacking District. *848 Washington St.; 877/550-4646 or 212/645-4646; standardhotels.com; doubles from $.*

WHERE TO STAY

1. Bowery Hotel From Sean MacPherson and Eric Goode, the duo behind the Waverly Inn, a 135-room brick structure with an atmospheric hotel bar. *335 Bowery; 212/505-9100; theboweryhotel.com; doubles from $$.*

2. Cooper Square Hotel Futuristic 21-story structure that soars above its gritty surroundings. *25 Cooper Square; 888/251-7979; thecoopersquarehotel.com; doubles from $$.*

KEY TO THE HOTEL PRICE ICONS   **$** UNDER $250   **$$** $250–$499   **$$$** $500–$749   **$$$$** $750–$999   **$$$$$** $1,000 AND UP

12. Minetta Tavern One of the most exclusive tables in town. *113 MacDougal St.; 212/475-3850; dinner for two* **XXX**.

13. Momofuku Ssäm Bar From ramen to pork buns, culinary whiz David Chang updates comfort food. *207 Second Ave.; 212/254-3500; dinner for two* **XXX**.

14. Pastis A McNally gem, popular with the *Sex and the City* set. *9 Ninth Ave.; 212/929-4844; dinner for two* **XXX**.

15. Russ & Daughters Legendary Jewish food emporium that might just offer the best bagel, lox, and cream-cheese combo in New York. *179 E. Houston St.; 212/475-4880; lunch for two* **X**.

16. Scarpetta Meatpacking District standout serving seasonal and savory Italian. *355 W. 14th St.; 212/691-0555; dinner for two* **XXX**.

17. Schiller's Liquor Bar Hipster hangout with surprisingly good food. *131 Rivington St.; 212/260-4555; dinner for two* **XXX**.

18. Soto Austere yet intimate Japanese restaurant. *357 Sixth Ave.; 212/414-3088; dinner for two* **XXX**.

19. Standard Grill The hot dining scene in the Meatpacking District; located in the Standard hotel. *848 Washington St.; 212/645-4100; dinner for two* **XXX**.

20. Waverly Inn & Garden Movie stars and millionaires all break bread in this low-ceilinged restaurant owned by *Vanity Fair's* Graydon Carter. *16 Bank St.; no phone; dinner for two* **XXX**.

21. WD-50 Unassuming East Village location and astonishing, out-of-the-box fare—from "aerated" foie gras to a playful take on cold fried chicken. *50 Clinton St.; 212/477-2900; dinner for two* **XXX**.

WHERE TO SHOP

22. Blue & Cream Everything from hoodies to high-end fashion. *1 E. First St.; 212/533-3088.*

23. Derek Lam Luxe ready-to-wear in a space-age setting. *12 Crosby St.; 212/966-1616.*

Russ & Daughters.

24. Freemans Sporting Club The preferred tailors of the bearded, plaid shirt–chic crowd. *8 Rivington St.; 212/673-3209.*

25. J.Crew's Liquor Store One-off, one-stop shop for the retro-hip gentleman. *235 W. Broadway; 212/226-5476.*

26. John Varvatos Flagship store on the site of rock club CBGB. *315 Bowery; 212/358-0315.*

27. Kiosk High-design knick-knacks from around the world. *95 Spring St.; 212/226-8601.*

28. Moss Industrial product design with a fashionable edge. *150 Greene St.; 212/204-7100.*

29. Opening Ceremony Sartorial trendsetters showcasing lines from around the globe. *35 Howard St.; 212/219-2688.*

30. Partners & Spade High-concept boutique and gallery space with an intriguing assortment of random merchandise. *40 Great Jones St.; 646/861-2827.*

NIGHTLIFE

31. Bowery Electric No-frills boîte lit with vintage lamps and serving up beer and rock and roll. *327 Bowery; 212/228-0228.*

32. Death & Co. Old-timey bar specializing in deftly mixed cocktails. *433 E. Sixth St.; 212/388-0882.*

33. (Le) Poisson Rouge Multi-performance space and bar in the former home of the iconic nightclub the Village Gate. *158 Bleecker St.; 212/505-3474; lepoissonrouge.com.*

34. Mayahuel East Village shrine to tequila and mescal. *304 E. Sixth St.; 212/253-5888.*

35. Milk & Honey Downtown's original hush-hush speakeasy. *134 Eldridge St.; milkandhoney reservations@gmail.com.*

36. Pegu Club Colonial-esque lounge with exotic house drinks. *77 W. Houston St.; 212/473-7348.*

37. The Stone Spartan space showcasing avant-garde music. *Corner of Second St. and Ave. C; no phone; thestone nyc.com.*

WHAT TO SEE + DO

High Line Elevated train track turned verdant park, with expansive views of Manhattan's West Side. *Entrances on Gansevoort St., 14th St.,16th St., 18th St., and 20th St.; 212/500-6035; thehighline.org.*

38. Lower East Side Tenement Museum Restored old-world apartments depicting the 19th-century immigrant experience. *91 Orchard St.; 212/431-0233; tenement.org.*

39. New Museum International contemporary art exhibitions in Downtown's boldest building. *235 Bowery; 212/219-1222; newmuseum.org.*

The High Line.

Five Great Late-Night Eats
Chef and restaurateur David Chang shares his favorite after-hours places to grab a bite.

40. Balthazar "There's nothing like getting a table with friends at midnight and pounding your way through a massive *plateau de fruits de mer.*" *80 Spring St.; 212/965-1414; dinner for two* **XXX**.

41. Blue Ribbon Brasserie "With a menu that spans everything from fried chicken and bone marrow to paella, this restaurant can please almost anyone." *97 Sullivan St.; 212/274-0404; dinner for two* **XXX**.

42. Great NY Noodletown "Open until four a.m. It's much more comforting to wake up with a receipt from this place in your pocket than a half-eaten pizza in your kitchen." *28 Bowery; 212/349-0923; dinner for two* **XX**.

43. PDT "Great drinks from Jim Meehan and Co. Hot dogs from Crif Dogs. Add a bed, and I think I've found my new apartment." *113 St. Marks Place; 212/614-0386; drinks for two* **XX**.

44. Spotted Pig "It's a bold move to offer sweetbreads at one a.m., but here it feels natural. They also have one of the city's best burgers and an unbelievable plate of *ricotta gnudi.*" *314 W. 11th St.; 212/620-0393; dinner for two* **XXX**.

KEY TO THE DINING PRICE ICONS **X** UNDER $25 **XX** $25–$74 **XXX** $75–$149 **XXXX** $150–$299 **XXXXX** $300 AND UP

49TH STATE OF MIND

THE CLASSIC ALASKA ITINERARY INCLUDES OVERSIZE MOUNTAINS, REMOTE FLY-IN LODGES, AND DRAMATIC FLOATPLANE RIDES—NOT TO MENTION GRIZZLY BEARS, GLACIERS, AND AN ENDLESS SUPPLY OF FRESH SALMON. GO INTO THE WILD FOR THE ULTIMATE ADVENTURE. BY JEFF WISE

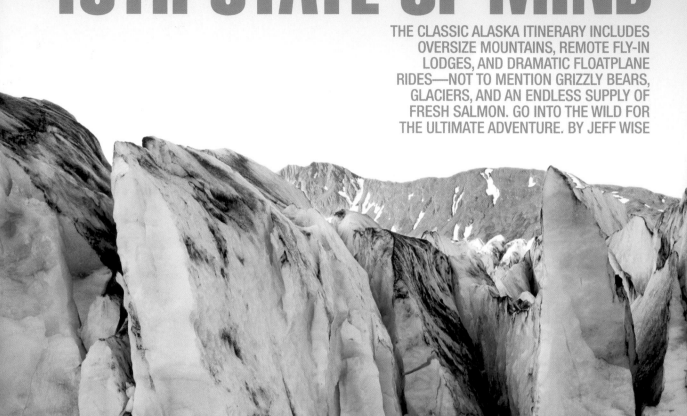

Photographed by Brown W Cannon III

Wilderness guide Amy Smith at the Redoubt Bay Lodge, in Alaska's Chigmit Mountains, west of Anchorage. OPPOSITE: The Colony Glacier, near the Alyeska Resort, in Girdwood.

THE PILOT EYED THE GATHERING CLOUDS AS HE TAXIED TO THE END OF LAKE HOOD,

the seaplane base that runs alongside Anchorage's international airport. We were hoping to get to Redoubt Bay Lodge, a tiny hideaway on the edge of a vast wilderness of rock and ice called the Chigmit Mountains, but above us, the low overcast was thickening. It was one of those Alaska moments: Should we push it or hold off? If we hesitated, we might be stuck in Anchorage until the weather cleared, and there was no telling how long that would be.

The clouds floated past, yellow and ragged. Overhead, a weak patch of blue appeared. The pilot gunned the engine, and the plane sat up on its haunches, then jumped into the air. We shouldered through the wispy clouds and up into the sky. The horizon was lined with snow-draped volcanoes.

My wife, Sandra, and I were off on the first leg of a 10-day summer trip to some of the state's most iconic destinations. Laying our plans, we'd ticked off all the features of the classic Alaskan itinerary: the fly-in lodge; grizzly bear and other wildlife sightings; fishing for salmon; a scenic railway journey; a backcountry trek in Denali National Park; a flight around the continent's highest peak, Mount McKinley; and then, to finish it all off, a power-down session at a luxury resort in the Chugach Mountains. In 10 days, we couldn't see all of Alaska, or even a modest fraction (it's more than twice the size of Texas). But we'd get a taste of what it has to offer, a roster of experiences the likes of which you can't find anywhere else in the country. It would be a brief, intense immersion in the alternate universe that is America's 49th state.

FIFTY MINUTES LATER, WE WERE FLYING OVER a bright blue lake hemmed in by an amphitheater of rugged emerald hills. In the farther distance, the fingers of innumerable glaciers descended the flanks of steep black mountains. The floatplane swooped down, settled onto the lake, and taxied toward a small dock. As we drew close, we could make out a cluster of log buildings in the surrounding forest. We had arrived at Redoubt Bay.

Fly-in lodges are key to the Alaska experience. Usually quite modest in scale, never done up with excess luxury, they are above all remote, so that by the time you get there you have a huge wilderness to yourself. Many of the best lodges started out as homesteading claims back in the 50's and 60's, when the government was giving Alaskan land to anyone who would build on it and live there. Redoubt Bay Lodge occupies a five-acre lot amid the 170,000 acres designated as the Redoubt Bay Critical Habitat Area, a state-managed preserve that, thanks in part to massive runs of salmon, is thick with bears.

Bear-watching was what we'd come for. Our guide, an endearingly ursine young man named Drew Hamilton, led us from the floatplane dock up along a path through the dense undergrowth to our cabin. "You're located right on a major bear path," he said as we arrived at the front steps. "If you see one, stand your ground. Say, 'Hey, bear!' and wave your hands."

Sandra looked uneasy.

"The important thing is," Hamilton cautioned, "if you see one, don't run."

The cabin was small but pleasant, with a cast-

OPPOSITE, CLOCKWISE FROM TOP LEFT: A floatplane landing; the rack of lamb at Redoubt Bay Lodge; cabins at the lodge; a Dolly Varden trout, caught in the south fork of the Big River, at Redoubt Bay.

iron stove and a view out over the lake. It did not seem particularly bear-proof. When it came time to go to dinner, I cracked the door open and craned my neck out. "It's like being in a zoo," Sandra said, "except we're in the cages, and the animals are roaming around."

Not for the first or last time, we were forced to confront Alaska's well-known potential for lethality. The state has been typecast as a land of fatal misadventures in such movies and books as *Grizzly Man, The Edge,* and *Into the Wild,* and in truth, the rep isn't exactly groundless. The state's tourism bureau has struggled to project a sunnier image. They shelved one of their slogans, Alaska B4UDie, a few years back, no doubt realizing it had slightly morbid overtones.

Summer days are long in the subarctic, and it was still light out when we returned to the main lodge and settled down to dinner. Kirsten Dixon, who owns the property with her husband, Carl, is something of a culinary celebrity in Alaska, and she

has made great strides in elevating the level of wilderness cooking. While exotic ingredients have to be flown in, there's incredible fresh bounty right at hand, ranging from salmon and halibut to berries and fiddlehead ferns, which Dixon regularly forages herself. For dinner we had salmon fillet pan-seared at high heat and finished with a balsamic glaze. Exquisitely prepared, it benefited from being the first of the countless salmon dishes we would eat during our trip.

For all the talk of bears, we hadn't actually seen one yet. The next day Sandra and I paddled across the lake with Hamilton to Wolverine Cove, a spot where a rushing creek empties into a shallow, cobble-bottomed inlet. As I sat very still in my kayak, a vast school of sockeye salmon swirled underneath, roiling the water so thickly that I practically could have walked over them. Three brown bears, a.k.a. grizzlies, loitered on the shore about 50 feet away—an adult female with two adolescent offspring. A smaller black bear appeared on the hillside above them and stood observing cautiously. Hamilton told us that this is one of the few areas in the world where brown and black bears interact regularly.

Slap! A two-foot-long salmon jumped clear of the water a few feet away. The juvenile brown bears waded out into the cove, prowling with their snouts in the water, plunging and splashing after the fleet-finned salmon. Their efforts brought them close enough that their splashes rocked my kayak. But they had no luck with the fish. "They're just having fun," Hamilton said. "When the salmon start running out of the lake and up into the stream, they'll be much easier for the bears to catch."

Over the next few days, we spin-cast for sockeye salmon, visited a waterfall, and took a jet boat up a shallow gravel-bedded river, then drifted down, watching the bald eagles watch us from their spruce-tree roosts. The last afternoon of our stay, I was sitting on the deck of the main lodge, examining the far shore for bears. I thought I spotted one in a bed of reeds, a black dot amid the beige. Just then, there was a clatter and shouting behind me. Two of the lodge's cooks were banging pans to shoo a bear off the kitchen porch. I turned to see a black streak scurry up the path toward our cabin and then dart off through the undergrowth.

We caught another floatplane back to Anchorage on our way to Denali National Park, the crown jewel of Alaska tourism. We passed over a pod of a hundred beluga whales cruising the coast of the Cook Inlet, their backs making long white ovals as they surfaced, then disappearing in the silty water.

To get to Denali, we would have to face a cruel reality of Alaskan travel: logistics. In a huge state with few roads, getting from A to B can require perseverance. The park itself is larger than Massachusetts, with only a single, unpaved road. No private cars are allowed, so you have to travel by bus. Along its entire length there are no services at all, only a handful of rustic lodges—ours was at the end, seven hours in. "Seven hours on a bus": the five most heartbreaking words in the English language for a traveler.

We spent the night at the Hotel Captain Cook, a wonderful relic of the pipeline-boom 70's—I half expected George Hamilton to leap out from behind the wood paneling. Then onward north, 7½ hours aboard the Alaska Railroad. We sat on one of the top-deck observation cars, where the glass roof and walls gave unobstructed views as we made our way over narrow gorges and swift-rushing streams, past steep valleys framed by craggy mountains.

The next morning we boarded the converted school bus that would take us into the park. Soon enough, as we drove along the gravel road we saw spread before us a broad tundra valley with the Alaska Range rising from the far side and, many miles in the distance, the grand white slab of Mount McKinley (also known as Denali) itself.

WE PASSED A POD OF A HUNDRED BELUGA WHALES CRUISING THE COAST, THEIR BACKS MAKING LONG WHITE OVALS AS THEY SURFACED

The passengers erupted in cheers. Because of the generally unpredictable weather in these parts and the mountain's great distance from the park entrance, many visitors never actually lay eyes on the tallest mountain in North America. So we could cross that worry off our list.

The High One—as its name translates from Athabascan—was soon hidden again behind intervening mountains as we wound up and down through a series of river valleys, climbing above the treeline to pass through areas of tundra with sweeping unobstructed views, then back down into spruce forest. Along the way we spotted a couple of grizzly bears, Dall sheep, countless caribou, snowshoe hares, and a lone wolf. Though Alaska is full of wilderness, the sheer scale of it here was awesome. Denali is the Alaska of Alaska—Alaska Squared, you could say.

At Camp Denali, we stayed in a one-room log cabin that stood by itself on a hillside, close enough to the main lodge for comfort and far enough for privacy. It had gingham curtains, a big wooden bed, and gas-powered lamps. And there, through the window above the writing desk, shone Mount McKinley, as clear and bright as the moon. Through

OPPOSITE, FROM FAR LEFT: On the Alaska Railroad, traveling from Anchorage to Denali National Park; the mountains near Girdwood, east of Anchorage.

TOP, FROM LEFT: Hiking near Wonder Lake, in Denali National Park; inside a cabin at Camp Denali; a mountain flower in bloom. BELOW: A Camp Denali vista.

ALASKANS SEEM TO HAVE A FEARLESS CONFIDENCE ABOUT THE NATURAL WORLD, EMBARKING ON SNOWMOBILE RACES AND SURFING IN FRIGID WATERS

a pair of binoculars, I watched the clouds whipping around the cornices and ice cliffs of the summit. Climbers consider Denali one of the most dangerous mountains in the world, combining extreme altitude with a near-Arctic latitude. For us it would simply be an infrequently recurring treat, like whale sightings on a long cruise.

ONE MORNING AT BREAKFAST WE GROGGILY nodded hello to the chipper couple across the table from us, Henry and Kathy Huntington, from the town of Eagle River, outside Anchorage. He was giving a series of lectures at the lodge about the tribes of the far north, where he travels frequently to record the local folkways.

That night, after a day spent vigorously hiking to the top of a nearby 1,800-foot-high ridge, Sandra and I attended Henry's slide show about the Inuit of the North Slope. He said he was often astonished at the sangfroid with which the Inuit dwell in their environment. "One time," he said, "they invited me to a picnic lunch out on an ice floe, where they passed the time fishing and chatting and eating. And I kept thinking, this floe could break off at any time, and we'll be in deep trouble. But they didn't mind at all. They figured if it happened, they'd deal with it. They've been living on the ice for thousands of years."

It's not just the Inuit—all Alaskans seem to have a fearless confidence about the natural world, embarking on 1,000-mile snowmobile races and surfing in the frigid waters of Turnagain Arm. They fly small planes in unheard-of numbers—1 in 60 is a pilot—and think nothing of landing them on beaches and sandbars.

Indeed, bush flying is essential to the Alaskan character. There are whole neighborhoods in which every backyard has a little dock with a floatplane tied up to it.

Here in Denali, the quintessential bush-flying experience is buzzing around the mountain and, weather permitting, landing on one of the glaciers that flow down its flanks. The day of our flight dawned, alas, overcast and rainy. We loaded up. I got in front, with Sandra and three other passengers in the back. Once we were all buckled in, the tail

Caribou antlers at Denali National Park, below.

seemed to be hanging low, so the pilot, Aine Roberts, got out and shifted a backpack from the tail compartment to the front seat. Much better.

Roberts took off and turned the plane toward Denali, in hopes that the clouds might open up and give us a route to sunnier altitudes. Instead, the weather got worse, and soon we were humming along in a steady drizzle. Visibility was bad and getting worse. I'd heard from an experienced bush pilot (he'd survived five crashes) that the cardinal

WE'D BEEN EXPOSED TO THE ALASKAN VIEW OF REALITY: UP HERE, WILDERNESS IS STILL A FORMIDABLE FORCE, ONE THAT'S NOT UNDER HUMAN CONTROL

rule of bush flying is never to lose sight of the terrain below you. This seemed particularly important when flying up a steep, jagged canyon, as we happened to be doing.

"The challenge out here is the weather," Roberts told me over the intercom. "It's always changing, and changing fast."

She banked steeply and pulled a 180. We passed through an even heavier rain shower, then emerged over a green valley and into sunshine. Denali was off the table, but I didn't care. I was happy to be flying low over magnificent valleys and peaks, including one rounded hilltop where a dozen Dall sheep milled as we passed overhead.

BACK IN ANCHORAGE, WE RENTED A CAR AND drove 40 minutes south to the town of Girdwood. Now that we'd survived Denali, it was time to relax.

Girdwood is the Palm Springs of Anchorage, the resort-town getaway where the state's glamorous elite—including former Alaska senator Ted Stevens, notoriously—have built mansion-size log cabins. The town is also notable as the home of the Alyeska Resort, the only hotel in the state to which the word *luxurious* can plausibly be applied. Built at great expense by Japan's Seibu conglomerate shortly before that country's real estate economy collapsed in the 1990's, it remains a monument to East-meets-West postmodern luxe.

A gondola runs from the back of the hotel up to the resort's own 2,500-foot-high ski mountain.

Sandra headed off for a massage while I took a long soak in the tub, then we reconvened to ride up to the mountaintop Seven Glaciers restaurant, a formal dining room with the best views in the state. It's famous in Alaska as a place to celebrate an anniversary or pop the question, and our fellow gondola passengers, all in their Sunday best, seemed positively giddy as we levitated above the valley floor. As were we. The sky was clearing. Sunshine spilled across snow in the gullies and bowls. We came to a stop at the top, and the conductor called out: "Be careful when leaving the tram—remember, you're on top of a mountain, in Alaska."

We stepped out onto the snow to take in the vista, avoided a fatal plunge, and made our way into the dining room. Our table seemed to hang precipitously over the lush valley, the fjordlike Turnagain Arm shimmering distantly in the late-summer light. In this refined setting, we felt both metaphorically and literally elevated above the drama and severity of Alaska. As I studied the menu, trying to choose between the mesquite-grilled elk loin and the mesquite-grilled-and-smoked Alaskan salmon, I felt like we were floating in a bubble.

And it *was* a bubble—the protective embrace of civilization, a reminder of the world to which we'd soon be returning. For the moment it felt odd. Something unexpected had happened to us over the course of our journey: we'd been exposed to a new perspective, the Alaskan view of reality. Here, wilderness is still a formidable force, one that's not under human control. You have to give up the idea that you are the top predator, that you are in charge of things. If you don't learn to treat the natural world with respect, you will be in real danger. But if you do, you'll see the world for what it is: a place where people are small and don't matter all that much. Living in our houses and riding in cars and planes in the Lower 48, we don't often glimpse that truth. In Alaska, you see it all the time.

The feeling would fade, I knew. But for now, as the setting sun touched the tips of the mountains, we were still in that Alaska mentality, that 49th state of mind.

OPPOSITE: Denali National Park, as seen from a plane, with Mount McKinley visible in the distance.

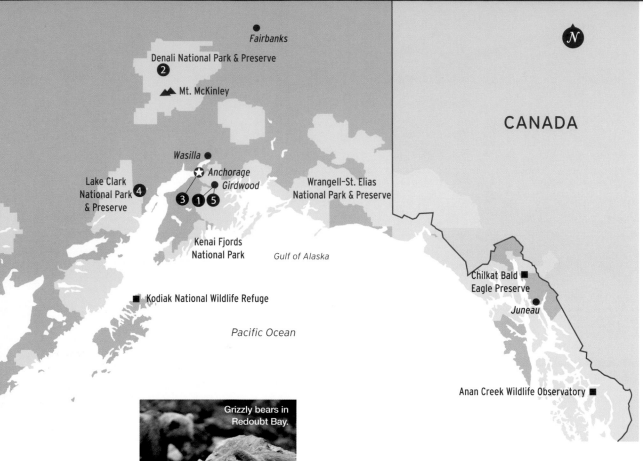

Fairbanks

Denali National Park & Preserve
②

▲ Mt. McKinley

CANADA

Wasilla ●

☆ Anchorage
● Girdwood

Lake Clark
National Park ④
& Preserve

③ ① ⑤

Wrangell–St. Elias
National Park & Preserve

Kenai Fjords
National Park   *Gulf of Alaska*

■ Kodiak National Wildlife Refuge

Chilkat Bald ■
Eagle Preserve

Juneau ●

Pacific Ocean

Anan Creek Wildlife Observatory ■

Grizzly bears in
Redoubt Bay.

WHEN TO GO
The best time to travel to Alaska
is late June through early
September, when it's relatively
warm with abundant daylight.

GETTING THERE +
AROUND
Anchorage is the most sensible
starting point; from there,
traveling between destinations
often means taking a ferry, train,
or plane—or all three. Depending
on the trip, it may make sense
to work with one of the outfitters
listed here.

TRIPS + TOUR OPERATORS
Abercrombie & Kent On A&K's
signature Alaska itinerary, travelers
can fly over Mount McKinley,
ride aboard Alaska Railroad's
GoldStar service, and meet a
champion Iditarod racer and his
dog-sledding team. *800/554-
7094; abercrombiekent.com; eight
days from $$$$$ per person.*
Mountain Travel Sobek
Known for small groups led by
local guides; excursions include
Discover Alaska, a multisport
journey through the southeast
that takes you on a cruise to
the humpback whale feeding
grounds at Point Adolphus.
*888/831-7526; mtsobek.com; six
days from $$$$$ per person.*
Off the Beaten Path Animal
life—sea lions, otters, whales,
and brown bears, to mention just
a few—takes center stage on a
southeastern Alaska trip that
includes visits to the Chilkat Bald
Eagle Preserve and Glacier Bay
National Park. *800/445-2995;
offthebeatenpath.com; seven days
from $$$$$ per person.*
Tauck Cruising Prince William
Sound, touring Denali and
Wrangell–St. Elias national parks,
and visiting with local totem pole
carvers are parts of the Grand
Alaska vacation. *800/468-2825;
tauck.com; 15 days from $$$$$
per person.*

KEY TO THE HOTEL PRICE ICONS $ UNDER $250 $$ $250–$499 $$$ $500–$749 $$$$ $750–$999 $$$$$ $1,000 AND UP

TRANSPORTATION

Alaska Railroad Book a 7½-hour ride from Anchorage to Denali National Park on the flagship *Denali Star* train, with its double-decker dome cars and upper-level outdoor viewing area. *800/544-0552; alaskarailroad. com; one-way fare from $.*

Alaska State Ferry For trips along the coast. *800/642-0066; ferryalaska.com.*

Kantishna Air Specializes in air charters for Camp Denali and other lodges. *907/683-1223; katair.com.*

Rust's Flying Service Flies to Redoubt Bay Lodge and other camps. *800/544-2299 or 907/243-1595; flyrusts.com.*

WHERE TO STAY

1. Alyeska Resort Luxury lodging in a resort town in the Chugach Mountains, 40 miles from Anchorage. *1000 Arlberg Ave., Girdwood; 800/880-3880 or 907/754-1111; alyeskaresort. com; doubles from $$.*

2. Camp Denali Lodging built of timber, on 67 acres of remote tundra overlooking Denali's snowcapped peaks. *Denali National Park; 907/683-2290; campdenali.com; doubles from $$$$$ for a three-night stay.*

3. Hotel Captain Cook High-rise city hotel with views of the Chugach Mountains. *939 W. Fifth Ave., Anchorage; 800/843-1950 or 907/276-6000; captaincook. com; doubles from $$.*

4. Redoubt Bay Lodge Finely appointed cabins within a bear habitat at the edge of the Chigmit Mountains, accessible only

Alaska Railroad.

by floatplane. *907/274-2710; withinthewild.com; doubles from $$$$$, all-inclusive, including round-trip floatplane transportation from Anchorage.*

WHERE TO EAT

5. Seven Glaciers Located at the top of Alyeska's aerial tramway; the dining room looks out over seven hanging glaciers, and the menu specializes in game and seafood. *907/754-2237; dinner for two* **XXXX**.

Alyeska Resort.

FIVE GREAT PLACES TO SPOT WILDLIFE

Anan Creek Wildlife Observatory
Reachable only by floatplane or boat, this forested swath contains one of the largest pink salmon runs in southeastern Alaska (a fact that's well known among the four-footed set). You'll spot river otters, mink, and brown bears, all from a protected observation platform. *fs.fed.us.*

Chilkat Bald Eagle Preserve
Due north of Juneau, this 48,000-acre spread of rivers and tributaries is home to more than 80 bald eagle nests. Go between October and January for what humans might call a massive family reunion—some 3,000 bald eagles flock here to dine on five species of salmon. *dnr.alaska. gov/parks.*

Denali National Park & Preserve
Encompassing more than 6 million acres (including Mount McKinley, the tallest mountain in North America), this is also one of the largest protected ecosystems on the globe. On summer bus trips and occasionally on ranger-led hikes, you might pass caribou, moose, and Dall sheep. *nps. gov/dena.*

Kenai Fjords National Park
Where glacial ice meets the Pacific Ocean at the very edge of the Kenai Peninsula, both land and sea creatures abound: look for orcas and humpback whales in the waters, and mountain goats and moose on the emerald mountains. *nps.gov/kefj.*

Kodiak National Wildlife Refuge
On Kodiak Island Archipelago, which shares its name with the brown bears that proliferate (at last count, there were some 2,300) in its 1.9 million acres, visitors commonly spot red foxes, ermine, and Sitka black-tailed deer. Improve your chances of seeing a bear by staying in one of the nine cabins. *kodiak.fws.gov.*

Downtown L.A.'s
Deco Eastern
Columbia Building.
OPPOSITE: Surfers at
Topanga Beach.

Photographed by Lisa Eisner

L.A. CONFIDENT

CALL IT THE NEW AUTHENTICITY. ALIVE WITH
NEW APPRECIATION FOR HISTORIC BUILDINGS,
REVITALIZED NEIGHBORHOODS, AND MODEST
ARTS, THE CITY OF FOREVER YOUNG IS
FLOUTING THE OLD CLICHÉS. BY M. G. LORD

PLAYING ALVY SINGER IN 1977'S *ANNIE HALL,* WOODY ALLEN FAMOUSLY DESCRIBED

Los Angeles as a place whose only cultural advantage is being able to make a right turn on red. More than 30 years later, the old chestnut lives on, but the notorious Manhattan propagandist has crossed over. A few years ago, Los Angeles Opera general director Plácido Domingo invited Allen to direct *Gianni Schicchi,* the comic third opera in Puccini's triple-bill *Il Trittico.* This happens to say much more about Los Angeles than it does about Woody Allen.

For as long as outsiders have jeered at L.A.— "shallow!" "phony!" "pathologically car-dependent!"—L.A. has fought back, if not always from a position of confidence. There was a *there* there even before I moved back to my hometown from New York a decade ago, but that didn't stop my East Coast friends from teasing me mercilessly. These days, I rarely hear the "cultural wasteland" slur, or any other slur, for that matter. One friend who used to sneer spent an entire February flaunting her invitation to the opening of the Broad Contemporary Art Museum at the Los Angeles County Museum of Art—not just a fun bash for an important Renzo Piano building but also, amazingly, a nonindustry hot ticket during Academy Awards week. Another friend asked me to get her tickets to the L.A. Opera's production of, you guessed it, *Il Trittico.*

In the land of quakes, one might hesitate to call anything earthshaking, but L.A.'s transformation from a patchwork of born-yesterday suburbs (where I grew up) to a real, unified city registers high on the cultural Richter scale. L.A. hasn't lost its great historical markers —a beach; a sign; those movie studios. It still has strip malls and housing tracts, but it also has

a booming downtown for the first time since the 1950's—whose population has nearly tripled (from 18,700 to 42,500) since 1999. The construction of new buildings there and elsewhere in the city has made Angelenos notice venerable, neglected ones—and, astonishingly, has helped stave off their decline. Quite simply, L.A. has awakened to its past—its stories, its people, its places.

Downtown, where I live, I like the way the flashy curves of Frank Gehry's Walt Disney Concert Hall underscore the elegant functionality of the Dorothy Chandler Pavilion across the street. Long home to the Oscars, and now to the L.A. Opera, the Midcentury treasure was designed by iconic L.A. architect Welton Becket, who created both Hollywood's cylindrical Capitol Records building and its geodesic Cinerama Dome. Although the dome was never threatened with destruction, it was very nearly obscured—by ArcLight, the state-of-the-art movie complex of which it is now a part. At the urging of the Los Angeles Conservancy, however, developers changed plans and kept its golf-ball dimples in view. Likewise, in 2006, the Griffith Observatory, a beacon on the south-facing slope of Mount Hollywood, added more than 40,000 square feet of exhibition space by burrowing into the hill beneath it—leaving its famous shell, site of the climax in *Rebel Without a Cause,* unscathed.

In L.A., which has long clung to the notion of unending youth, a quiet, organic movement has emerged from finding value in the old. The mantra is "adaptive reuse." Its bugbears are disposability, fast food, and big carbon footprints. Its mascots are both a Prius (fueled at the all-green-but-the-

OPPOSITE, FROM TOP: The 1935 Griffith Observatory, which received an underground expansion; the lobby of the Dorothy Chandler Pavilion.

gas Helios House BP station) and an ancient diesel Mercedes—modified at Lovecraft Bio-Fuels, a company in Silver Lake, to run on doughnut grease.

This movement is not about preservation or conservation per se. It's about stewardship—of buildings and neighborhoods that carry history, and of passed-down skills. You could call it the New Authenticity, though some trend-watcher may very well coin a catchier phrase. L.A. resident Lisa Eisner, who photographed this story, is a Geiger counter for detecting it, and she led me to many exemplars. "I like things that avoid the 'Hollywood' cliché," she explained, "things that you can't find in other cities." The fashion world provides the first stop on what I'll call the New Authenticity tour.

Designer Christina Kim's company, Dosa, is synonymous with unbleached organic cotton,

environmentally friendly dyes, and recycled materials. In her factory in Downtown's Fashion District, Kim collects fabric scraps that would ordinarily be discarded. "I remember being amazed and fascinated at my grandmother's traditional Korean socks," she told me, describing soles patched with cotton cloth clipped from bedding, each piece a different shade of white. Mending, Kim realized, could "increase an object's value, especially when done by hand and with care." She went on to build a worldwide business by transforming fashion-industry detritus into luscious, labor-intensive clothes.

You can see Kim's designs on fans like Nicole Kidman and Jennifer Aniston and buy them at the L.A. Barneys. But to get a sense of her relationship to Los Angeles, you must see dosa818, her retail space on the 12th floor of the Wurlitzer Building, a terra-cotta–tiled gem on Downtown's Broadway. The 7,000-square-foot loft could easily be mistaken for a Zendo, were it not for the art installations and racks of gossamer clothes.

Kim relies on the skills behind the traditional arts and crafts of Latin America, where most of her workers come from, and she knows the immigrant experience firsthand: she came to Los Angeles with her family from South Korea when she was 15. And even though she later moved to New York City and established her flagship store there, she has always made her clothing here because of the workers. In 1994, she decided to move back. This was shortly after the acquittal of four white Los Angeles police officers—whose brutal beating of African American resident Rodney King was caught on videotape—led to widespread street violence. The verdict deepened the divide between prosperous, mostly white neighborhoods in the west and poorer, mostly black and Latino ones in the east, which the post–World War II suburban movement and the 1965 race riots in Watts had already begun to create.

"The King riot was part of what made me want to move back," Kim said. She wanted to participate in the healing process, "to bridge the gap—in a small way." Now she often works alongside her seamstresses—mending more than fabric in the once-simmering neighborhood.

Helios House, the LEED-certified BP gas station at the corner of Olympic and Robertson Boulevards, below.

SINCE 2000, MOST OF L.A.'S FAMOUSLY disconnected and derelict neighborhoods not only have rebounded but also have begun to cohere—with the millennium real estate bubble providing an unlikely glue. (Never mind that it has since popped.) Because many first-time home buyers could not afford West L.A.—often the place where they grew up—they turned east, resurrecting houses with "good bones" in Hollywood, Silver Lake, Los Feliz, and Echo Park. Many of my friends—to say nothing of L.A.'s closest culture watchers—were either party or witness to this. They lived next to different types of people and usually figured out how to get along. Home ownership changed these buyers, even the jaded ones who planned merely to flip. They learned respect for craftsmanship and hands-on work. They learned to value authenticity, and that began to inform their lives.

If any event serves as a rallying cry for authenticity, it is the loss of Mid-Wilshire's 84-year-old Ambassador Hotel, site of Robert Kennedy's assassination, which the city bulldozed in 2006 to make way for a school. Its legendary nightclub, the Cocoanut Grove, was slated to become an auditorium, but in 2008 it, too, was razed. As the hotel demolition began, three disillusioned preservationists threw a public wake in the Gaylord Hotel, across the street: L.A. Conservancy executive director Linda Dishman, Conservancy board member Diane Keaton, and club owner Andrew Meieran, who was then transforming an abandoned power plant into the Edison bar. "You could see the dust and hear the wrecking crew," Meieran said, still bitter at the recollection.

Meieran cut his preservationist teeth at UC Berkeley, where he lost the dormitory lottery but scraped together funds for a beat-up Craftsman bungalow, on which he learned the art of restoration. The Edison, which Meieran co-owns with Marc Smith, is now one of the hottest clubs in Downtown. In the room that gives the club its

Clothing designer Christina Kim at dosa818, her Downtown L.A. outpost, above. ON THE WALL: An installation of pieced-mica silhouettes of feet by Oaxacan artist Francisco Toledo.

THE CULT SPECTACLE *LUCHA VAVOOM* IS A CHAOTIC MINGLING OF BURLESQUE DANCERS, MASKED MEXICAN WRESTLERS, AND LOWRIDER CARS

name, a gigantic, rivet-covered, cast-iron generator makes you feel like a stowaway in the engine room of a Jules Verne submarine. The old equipment still hums with the promise of its time. "A hundred years ago," Meieran said, "people had just discovered how to harness electricity, record voices, and transmit radio."

A mile from the Edison, the Orpheum Theatre—a walnut-walled vaudeville-era space—occupies a stretch of Broadway that once had 12 movie houses and three major department stores. Most were shuttered, and the street was eerily dead at night when Dishman became executive director of the L.A. Conservancy in 1992. "There was no crime, though," she says, "because there were no people to commit crimes against." Building on efforts begun in 1978, when the Conservancy was formed, activist citizens such as Meieran and fellow bar owner Cedd Moses, developers including Tom Gilmore (an early evangelist for Downtown), and the city itself have taken Broadway off life support. Lyle Lovett, Alanis Morissette, and other performers now play at the Orpheum. It's also one of the historic movie houses that host the Last Remaining Seats, a Conservancy program screening vintage movies to support such ongoing projects as the restoration of Frank Lloyd Wright's 1924 Ennis House, in Los Feliz. Near the Orpheum, the restored Mayan Theater is known for its triannual cult spectacle *Lucha Vavoom*, a chaotic mingling of burlesque dancers, masked *lucha libre* Mexican wrestlers (inspiration for Jack Black's movie *Nacho Libre)*, and lowrider cars. With skulls painted on their faces and tights as good as painted on their thighs, the wrestlers are a balance of earnestness and goofiness.

L.A. has never stopped celebrating its longest-running raison d'être, and film societies such as American Cinematheque, the grande dame headquartered in the 1922 Egyptian Theatre, lure people out of their living rooms with fare that goes far beyond Turner Classic Movies. Since 2001, the hip Cinespia has projected films onto a mausoleum wall, "above and below the stars," in the Hollywood Forever Cemetery. To compensate for the modest irreverence of allowing fans to picnic on the graves, part of its $10 admission fee goes to restoring the grounds.

The Cinefamily, the relatively new kid on the film-society block, projects films in the Silent Movie Theatre, a landmark 1942 structure in the Fairfax District that may be best known for the grisly murder of its owner there in 1997. Brothers Sammy and Dan Harkham, who grew up in the neighborhood, bought the theater three years ago and hired programmer Hadrian Belove to build a series equal to that of American Cinematheque. They wanted to expand beyond silent films, but not abandon them—or the legacy of the theater's 96-year-old organist, Bob Mitchell, who passed away last year.

AMOEBA MUSIC, ON SUNSET BOULEVARD IN Hollywood near the ArcLight, is one of several singular stores on our tour. It is a monument to vinyl, an emblem of the once indomitable record industry as it pretzels into an iTunes world. The L.A. branch of a Berkeley-based store, Amoeba carries 250,000 titles. Shopping here is as much about touch and sight as about hearing—placing your fingers on CD's and record albums, responding viscerally to seductive cover art, whose importance has been diminished by digital distribution.

While Amoeba preserves the vanishing pleasure of record shopping, Family, a bookstore on Fairfax, is building a bulwark against the iPad and Kindle. The shop's back wall is papered with a blown-up black-and-white photo of a gun-toting Eastern European Jewish vigilante group formed to guard against pogroms. Co-owner David Jacob Kramer bills Family as "a curated bookstore." This means that it stocks very few books, but for each of its pristine copies there is one dog-eared version that Kramer or his business partner, the aforementioned Silent Movie Theatre's Sammy Harkham, has read and loved. For the store to function, you have to trust them—to believe that because you and they both like, say, Mikhail Bulgakov's classic *The Master and Margarita,* you will also like David Shrigley's *Ants Have Sex in Your Beer.* Apparently trust keeps the place open. "Our clients have become our friends," said Kramer, whose friends range from *Simpsons* creator Matt Groening to "70-year-old guys who used to write for *Star Trek.*"

The Silent Movie Theatre, in Mid-Wilshire, above. OPPOSITE: Staffers Erick Vindel and Aimee Pinga at Hollywood's Amoeba Music.

The Echo Park Time Travel Mart, on Sunset Boulevard, has been designed to resemble a 1970's 7-Eleven. Yet instead of Slurpees, Pringles, and aspirin, it sells dinosaur eggs, robot milk, and "leeches—nature's tiny doctors." The more you look, the weirder it gets: LOST: DECADE announces a sign on the bulletin board. HAVE YOU SEEN 1960–70? ANY INFO WOULD BE HELPFUL. LAST SEEN IN MY FRIEND STEVE'S VAN. It may take a minute, but then the visitor gets it. This is a put-on—an art installation: a convenience store stocked for a road trip through time. But the merchandise sells, and almost as soon as the store opened in the spring of 2008, it earned enough to pay rent for the nonprofit walk-in tutoring center for neighborhood kids, called 826LA, that occupies the rest of the building.

Both store and center are the brainchildren of Dave Eggers, author and publisher of the *McSweeney's* literary journal, who started the first such concern in San Francisco in 2002. To make the Echo Park space possible, *40-Year-Old Virgin* producer Judd Apatow hosted a parody fund-raiser, "An Evening of Best Intentions," honoring actor Seth Rogen for "the charity work he is considering doing in the future." Apatow exacted tributes from actors Will Ferrell, Ben Stiller, and dozens of others, Eggers told me. "Guests were given Kentucky Fried Chicken to eat and the décor was borrowed from the *Rocky Balboa* premiere held a few days earlier," he said. "It was a wild and hilarious night."

Ordinarily this would be a hard act to follow, but not if you have a time machine. On the heels of the party, 826LA's then executive director, Mac Barnett, booked readings by dead authors (okay, dead-author impersonators) Homer, Steinbeck, and Emily Dickinson. "We're finally going to get her out of the house," he joked.

UNTIL RECENTLY, A DICKINSON TYPE IN Downtown's Arts District could have stayed happily indoors—with no galleries or bistros to

tempt her. But today my still-gritty neighborhood houses lofts and restaurants like R23, whose exceptional Japanese food has drawn locals and adventurous West Siders since 1991.

Like those in New York City's SoHo, the district's vacant warehouses were colonized by artists starting in the late 1960's, but as the area gentrified, rents rose—sending artists to newer urban frontiers like Boyle Heights. MOCA's Temporary Contemporary took up residence in nearby Little Tokyo in 1983. It is now permanently the Geffen Contemporary. Some remaining battered buildings in the city's historic core are its newest places to view art—pulling the Chinatown art crowd to 30 galleries, mostly on Main and Spring Streets, which were dubbed Gallery Row by the city in 2003. The Downtown Art Walk draws about 4,000 people, ranging from artists to West L.A. collectors.

One of the most collectible artists is a pioneer of an industrial section of Boyle Heights, across the Los Angeles River: painter Amy Bessone,

whose work has been bought by MOCA. Bessone is best known for her large-scale paintings of Meissen porcelain figurines rendered as if they were alive. "There is a strange moment in the porcelains where German folklore meets Disney," she told me. Of the new work in her studio, she said, "The last porcelains I painted were close-ups of faces. Their surfaces were very masklike, which drew me to painting masks themselves."

IF LOS ANGELES IS COMING INTO ITS OWN, it's because it is learning to embrace the contradictions that define any great city. Downtown's Deco Eastern Columbia Building, a turquoise jewel converted to condominium lofts (Johnny Depp owns a penthouse), is a far cry from neighboring South Park—a cluster of glittering new residential skyscrapers near the Staples Center, home of the L.A. Lakers. And Clifton's Brookdale Cafeteria—opened in 1935 as a haven from the Great Depression—is a far cry from just about everything else.

If Mad King Ludwig of Bavaria had decided to open a cafeteria and pattern it after a hunting lodge, Clifton's would be it. Columns disguised as redwoods appear to poke through the dining room ceiling. A 20-foot waterfall washes through its center. Long before feng shui made it to the States, founder Clifford Clinton knew that the sound of water was soothing. "My grandfather's parents were missionaries in China," said

IN A CITY THAT HAS LONG CLUNG TO THE NOTION OF UNENDING YOUTH, A MOVEMENT HAS EMERGED FROM FINDING VALUE IN THE OLD

Clifford's grandson, restaurant manager Robert Clinton. As a little boy, Clifford saw hunger, poverty, and hopelessness. When he had a chance to alleviate them, he jumped at it. "He wanted a place where people could leave all that outside and eat good, wholesome, low-priced food," Clinton said. Even at Broadway's lowest point, Clifton's never closed its doors. "We are a landmark. We don't need a plaque on the door to say so."

Neither does another living landmark, Bob Baker, who carves marionettes and trains apprentices to animate them a mile and a half northwest, in Filipinotown. Baker gave his first puppet show at age eight, in 1933, and has been mounting them ever since. With its houselights on, the theater is nothing. With the lights down, it's unforgettable—part Ice Capades, part Muppets, part Chinese opera, part Bolshoi Ballet. And you see the puppeteers, a rainbow of ethnicities, walking among the audience, hands flying, convincing you that the marionettes are alive and the humans are struggling to keep up with them. Even before the theater was founded in 1963, Baker, who worked in movies, was a hit with Hollywood families. "Poor little Liza Minnelli," he recalled. "She was always getting left behind. She used to put her arms around me and say, 'I love you, puppet man.'" Some kids who celebrated their sixth birthdays in the theater are coming back to celebrate their fortieth.

PLÁCIDO DOMINGO GETS IT THAT authenticity is not about snubbing community; it's why he's tapped Hollywood heavies Garry Marshall, William Friedkin, and Woody Allen to direct. It's why the L.A. Opera performs free for kids, and why it has commissioned a work on Rafael Mendez, who as a boy played trumpet in Pancho Villa's army and as a man performed with the MGM Orchestra. "How are we going to get people to love our religion," Domingo once asked a staff member, "if we don't invite them into the church?"

When Welton Becket designed the original 1964 Music Center complex, anchored on the south by the Chandler Pavilion, he made a controversial decision—to raise its plaza above street level. Becket's L.A. was not pedestrian-friendly, so the placement of the plaza did not seem outrageous. But L.A. is rethinking its symbiosis with the car: when gas prices spiked in the summer of 2007, so did ridership on the L.A. Metro—which includes the Red Line, a 17-mile-long subway that makes it possible to travel from Downtown to the San Fernando Valley without hitting traffic. It may also be time to rethink Becket's symbolic placement of high art above the culture of the street.

The 110 Project, a work in progress commissioned by the L.A. Opera, may well erase that symbolic separation. It is a paean to the city's first freeway, the redoubtable I-110, which turned 70 in 2009. Emmy Award–winning Angeleno composer Laura Karpman wrote the score. Its libretto incorporates themes from "story circles"— public interviews held in the racially diverse neighborhoods that the freeway traverses. And it runs 110 minutes—the time it takes in heavy traffic to get from San Pedro (at one end of the city) to Pasadena (at the other).

"It's about moving not only from one place to another, but through time," said Stacy Brightman, the opera's director of community programs. It's about the wind in your hair and the right turn on red. "Seventy years—a lifetime. How has Los Angeles changed in a lifetime?"

And will it take a freeway or a subway into the future?

OPPOSITE: The front window of Family bookstore, in Fairfax.

GUIDE TO LOS ANGELES

Clifton's Brookdale Cafeteria.

London West Hollywood.

hearty, inexpensive fare in an unabashedly kitschy, woodland-inspired setting. *648 S. Broadway; 213/627-1673; dinner for two* ✗.

7. The Edison Atmospheric Downtown nightclub located in a former power plant. *108 W. Second St.; 213/613-0000; drinks for two* ✗✗.

8. The Must Cheerful wine bar and gastropub that specializes in small-production vintages and craft beers. *118 W. Fifth St.; 213/627-1162; dinner for two* ✗✗.

9. R23 Serene Japanese restaurant in a converted warehouse; a longtime neighborhood favorite. *923 E. Second St.; 213/687-7178; dinner for two* ✗✗✗.

10. Wurstküche Boisterous beer hall serving superlative artisanal sausages, which range from mango-jalapeño to exotic blends like rattlesnake-rabbit. *800 E. Third St.; 213/687-4444; dinner for two* ✗.

WHERE TO SHOP
11. Amoeba Music More than 250,000 titles on CD and vinyl. *6400 Sunset Blvd.; 323/245-6400; amoeba.com.*

12. Dosa818 Loft atelier and boutique for fashion designer Christina Kim's line, crafted with organic fabrics, environmentally friendly dyes, and recycled

by Benjamin Noriega-Ortiz. *8440 Sunset Blvd.; 800/697-1791 or 323/650-8999; morganshotelgroup.com; doubles from $$.*

3. Standard, Downtown L.A. Easily the district's trendiest hotel, courtesy of André Balazs, and located in the Modernist Superior Oil headquarters. *550 S. Flower St.; 866/670-8686 or 213/892-8080; standardhotel.com; doubles from $$.*

WHERE TO EAT + DRINK
4. Broadway Bar Art Deco watering hole next to the Orpheum Theatre. *830 S. Broadway; 213/614-9909; drinks for two* ✗.

5. Church & State Bustling, sophisticated bistro set on an old loading dock in Downtown and helmed by chef Walter Manzke. *1850 Industrial St.; 213/405-1434; dinner for two* ✗✗✗.

6. Clifton's Brookdale Cafeteria Depression-era landmark serving

WHERE TO STAY
1. London West Hollywood In the 2010 edition of the T+L 500, *Travel + Leisure* readers rated this the top property in California. *1020 N. San Vicente Blvd.; 866/282-4560 or 310/854-1111; thelondonwesthollywood.com; doubles from $.*

2. Mondrian Philippe Starck's signature look has been updated

Echo Park Time Travel Mart.

materials. *818 S. Broadway, 12th floor; 213/489-2801; dosainc.com.*

13. Echo Park Time Travel Mart
Market with an art installation that mimics a 1970's 7-Eleven, with dinosaur eggs and robot milk for sale. *1714 W. Sunset Blvd.; 213/413-3388.*

14. Family From coffee-table art tomes to graphic novels and obscure 'zines, this highly curated bookstore eschews mass appeal for the lo-fi, underground tastes of its owners. *436 N. Fairfax Ave.; 323/782-9221; familylosangeles.com.*

WHAT TO SEE + DO
15. Bob Baker Marionette Theater Puppet extravaganza that's part Muppets, part Bolshoi Ballet. *1345 W. First St.; 213/250-9995; bobbakermarionettes.com; $20.*

16. Broad Contemporary Art Museum At the Los Angeles County Museum of Art; three-story gallery designed by Renzo Piano and devoted to works from 1945 to the present. *5905 Wilshire Blvd.; 323/857-6000; lacma.org.*

Downtown Art Walk Popular monthly event brings together open galleries, local bands, vendors, performance art, a traveling circus, and some of the best food trucks in town.

Every second Thursday, 12–9 p.m.; free admission; downtownartwalk.com.

17. Downtown Independent Sleek, modern indie movie theater with stadium seating and an eclectic lineup; also hosts rooftop parties with live DJ's. *251 S. Main St.; 213/617-1033; downtownindependent.com.*

Gallery Row Pedestrian-friendly strip of exhibition spaces and cultural venues; the setting for the Downtown Art Walk. *Between Second and Ninth Sts. and Main and Spring Sts.*

18. Geffen Contemporary at MOCA Former warehouse redesigned by Frank Gehry and typically used for exhibitions of large-scale and more recent works. *152 N. Central Ave; 213/626-6222; moca.org.*

19. Griffith Observatory Landmark 1935 planetarium in Griffith Park, featured in *Rebel Without a Cause; Beverly Hills, 90210;* and many other films and television shows. *2800 E. Observatory Rd.; 213/473-0800; griffithobservatory.org.*

20. Los Angeles Opera at the Dorothy Chandler Pavilion Led by general director Plácido Domingo. *135 N. Grand Ave.; 213/972-7219; laopera.com.*

21. *Lucha Vavoom* Mexican-style wrestling meets stand-up comedy and burlesque, staged

at the historic Mayan Theater. *1038 S. Hill St.; 213/746-4674; luchavavoom.com.*

22. Museum of Contemporary Art (MOCA) More than 5,000 works of American and European art dating from 1940 to the present. *250 S. Grand Ave.; 213/626-6222; moca.org.*

23. Orpheum Theatre Once a vaudeville venue; now the site of film festivals, awards shows, and rock concerts. *842 S. Broadway; 877/677-4386; laorpheum.com.*

24. Walt Disney Concert Hall Iconic Frank Gehry architecture and world-class acoustics at the home of the L.A. Philharmonic. *111 S. Grand Ave.; 323/850-2000; laphil.com.*

The Dorothy Chandler Pavilion.

Underground Reading List

David Jacob Kramer of Family bookstore shares five of his favorite indie titles.

Buck Shots by Peter Sutherland *(PowerHouse Books, 2007, $29.95)* Oddly engrossing photographs of deer.

Idea Art for Kids by Mark A. Rodriguez *(self-published, 2006, $8)* Simple yet high-concept art projects for all ages.

New Painting and Drawing by Ben Jones *(PictureBox, 2008, $20)* Vibrant, almost psychedelic collection of visual works from a young artist on the rise.

1-800-MICE by Matthew Thurber *(self-published, $5)* Alt-comic series as complex and well-plotted as any gripping novel.

Wide Eyed by Trinie Dalton *(Akashic Books, 2005, $14.95)* Dreamlike short stories populated by memorable characters and sharp, intimate reflections.

FOR TRUE CINEMA BUFFS
Five film societies turn the moviegoing experience into a marquee event.

American Cinematheque Year-round films and retrospectives, primarily at the legendary Egyptian Theatre. *6712 Hollywood Blvd.; 323/466-3456; americancinematheque.com.*

ArcLight Hollywood Cinerama Dome Geodesic-domed theater built in 1963 and refurbished as part of the ArcLight Hollywood movie complex. *6360 W. Sunset Blvd.; 323/464-1478; arclightcinemas.com.*

The Cinefamily Newer society with screenings at the restored Silent Movie Theatre. *611 N. Fairfax Ave.; 323/655-2510; cinefamily.org.*

Cinespia Alfresco screenings on the lawn of the Hollywood Forever Cemetery; movies are projected onto the wall of a mausoleum that contains Rudolph Valentino's tomb. *6000 Santa Monica Blvd.; 323/469-1181; cinespia.org.*

Last Remaining Seats Summer series of vintage films and live entertainment screened in historic theaters. *For locations, call 213/623-2489 or visit laconservancy.org.*

KEY TO THE DINING PRICE ICONS   **X** UNDER $25   **XX** $25–$74   **XXX** $75–$149   **XXXX** $150–$299   **XXXXX** $300 AND UP

A ski break
on Buttermilk's
9,900-foot summit.

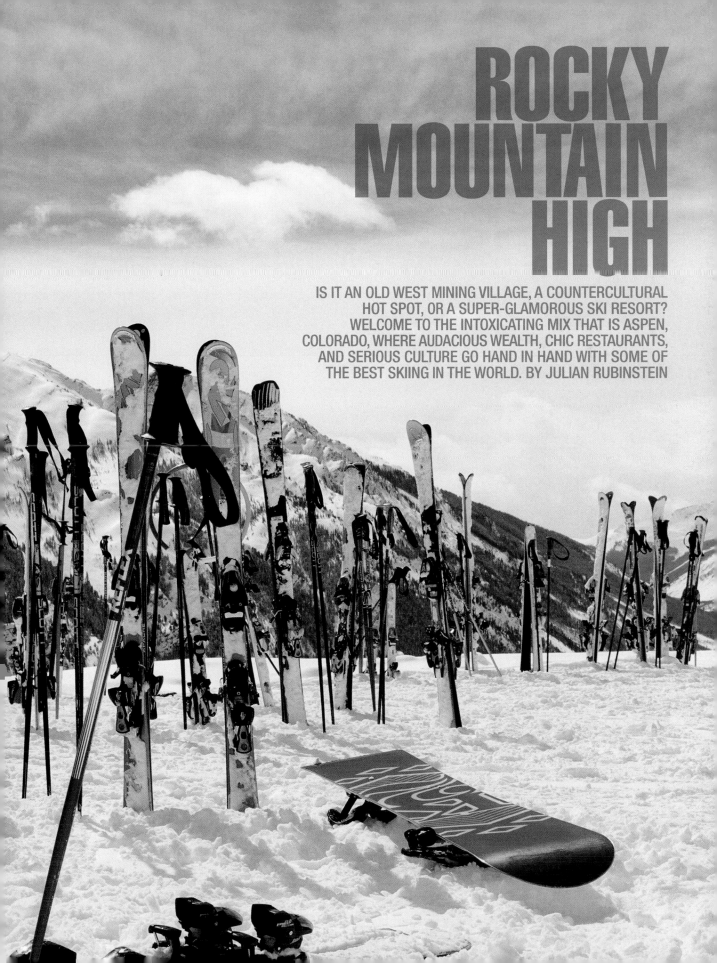

ROCKY MOUNTAIN HIGH

IS IT AN OLD WEST MINING VILLAGE, A COUNTERCULTURAL HOT SPOT, OR A SUPER-GLAMOROUS SKI RESORT? WELCOME TO THE INTOXICATING MIX THAT IS ASPEN, COLORADO, WHERE AUDACIOUS WEALTH, CHIC RESTAURANTS, AND SERIOUS CULTURE GO HAND IN HAND WITH SOME OF THE BEST SKIING IN THE WORLD. BY JULIAN RUBINSTEIN

IT'S AROUND LUNCHTIME IN ASPEN'S ROARING FORK VALLEY, AND I'D LIKE

nothing more than to tell you where I'm spending the afternoon. Only I can't, because—as I myself have just accepted—I don't know. I spent the past 40 minutes riding in the back of a Sno-Cat (fine) and then hiking (skis strapped to my back, but also fine) up the spine of a 12,392-foot peak. The so-called plan, known only to me, was to ski down the legendary Highland Bowl and then celebrate my accomplishment in, at minimum, a bar-serviced hot tub. This notion, however, appears to have been predicated on my live arrival at the summit, and as the panoramic Rocky Mountain–top view I have been enjoying disappears into a dark snow cloud, I soberly recall that my expedition began at the suggestion of an *Aspen Times* sex columnist whose dog, I knew damned well, was on the antidepressant Lexapro.

The wind whooshes and I steady myself with my poles, trying to enjoy the bitter cold. The thin ridge I'm ascending falls off so precipitously on either side that a few minutes ago, I couldn't bear to look down. Now I have no choice. All I can see is my own lumbering ski-boot tracks. One unfortunate tilt to the left or right and the phrase *early retirement* takes on a whole new meaning.

LIFE-THREATENING WAS NOT WHAT I HAD in mind when I planned my trip to Aspen. Then again, I was, upon my departure, between apartments and living out of a Manhattan Mini Storage unit. Aspen, I thought, promised something safe and familiar, a respite. It was a place I'd been going to since I was a child in Denver in the 1970's. There were lots of beautiful destinations within striking distance, but Aspen, in the eyes of many Denverites, was not only the most picturesque mountain town around, but also the most authentic. Unlike resorts that were erected for ski tourism,

such as Vail or Breckenridge, Aspen has real history in the 19th-century American West. In 1893 it was the nation's silver-mining capital, with six newspapers and a population of 12,000, when it went bust after the repeal of the Sherman Silver Purchase Act (which had briefly switched the country's monetary standard from gold to silver). Remnants of that era still exist in the limestone buildings that line the downtown streets, and in the splintered Smuggler's Mine chutes outside town where I used to climb.

As I became, by some measures, an adult, I continued to return to Aspen, and it was always the first place that came to mind whenever I was asked to name my favorite spot in the world. Usually I went in the summers, camping and hiking for several days in the shadow of the purple-hued Maroon Bells mountains and then returning to town to partake of the wonders of plumbing and the excellent classical music put on by the Aspen Music Festival. Aspen, for me, was always a place of contrasts: rugged and pristine, sophisticated and simple.

But as the years went by, I began to notice that more and more people had their own opinions about Aspen, and invariably they were quite different from mine. While I continued to see Aspen as the eccentric, arts- and civic-minded town where Hunter S. Thompson once ran for sheriff, promising he wouldn't take mescaline on duty, the wealth and celebrity Aspen had attracted since the days I started going—from Jack Nicholson to the Saudi Prince Bandar—created the impression that Aspen was like a Beverly Hills in the hills. The truth was, I thought, as my flight began its vertiginous descent into the snow-covered valley, I hadn't been back in several years, and I had no idea what I would find.

OPPOSITE: The whirlpool at Aspen Meadows Resort, with a view of Smuggler Mountain.

WHEN I STEPPED ONTO THE TARMAC, THE late afternoon sun was bathing the valley in a pink-and-gold light. Behind me, the windows of the multimillion-dollar houses on Red Mountain glinted like diamonds. Along the edges of the airfield, snow was piled easily 10 feet high. This was a disquieting reminder that it had already been a historic ski season. (So much snow had fallen that the town had to hire trucks to cart it away. "I've been here 30 years and I've never seen a winter in which people actually said, 'No more,'" Lon Winston, the director of the Thunder River Theatre Company, told me.) Disquieting, I say, because in my rush to get out here, I'd neglected to pack anything to ski in.

"Correct," I said into my cell phone, to a man I'd been referred to. "Pants, gloves, hat, goggles, jacket. I have nothing."

"No worries," the voice on the other end said. "See you in 15 minutes."

I hopped the shuttle to my hotel on the outskirts of town, the Aspen Meadows Resort. A sprawling property designed in Bauhaus style, Aspen Meadows is best known as the home of the venerable Aspen Institute. Founded in 1950, the institute has—especially in the almost four years since its president, Walter Isaacson, inaugurated the Ideas Festival—vaulted to the top rung of world conferences, filling the town each summer with more VIP's and plainclothes security men than an underground bunker during the apocalypse. Bill Clinton, the Dalai Lama, and Jordan's Queen Noor are among the hundreds of luminaries who have passed through for public panels and talks under the same white tent that the Music Festival uses for its performances. When you throw in the Aspen Santa Fe Ballet, Jazz Aspen Snowmass, and the Aspen Writers' Foundation, no place in the world remotely as small as Aspen (population 6,000) can boast such high-powered cultural institutions. I was pondering this outside the spectacularly designed

Doerr-Hauser event and art space when a Jeff Spicoli–style van pulled up in front of me, and out jumped a sunburned, long-maned man wearing ski pants and a black turtleneck. "Sorry I'm late," said Lorenzo Semple III, shaking my hand. "You caught me right as I was coming off the Bowl. Absolutely epic." He slid open the van door, revealing two hanging racks of ski apparel. "Suit Yourself," he said, stating the name of his business. *Aha*, I thought: *I've arrived.*

As I assembled an outfit, Semple and I covered an array of topics I'd never found so riveting—for example, lawn mowing, which he does all summer. Semple was dramatic in a good way, a true enthusiast, and it didn't surprise me to learn that he is the son of legendary screenwriter Lorenzo Semple Jr. *(Three Days of the Condor)*, the man he calls "my hero," and who first brought him to Aspen more than 30 years ago. Semple still has some Hollywood in him—he ended a cell-phone conversation with a phonetic kiss, "Mwah"—and I couldn't help but think he perfectly embodied the grit and glamour that make Aspen so unique. "I have two religions," he said. "Mountain biking and skiing. This year my goal is to get 200 runs on the Bowl. So far I'm at 152."

EVERYWHERE I WENT, PEOPLE WERE TALKING about "the Bowl"—which, in an outdoor fantasyland like Aspen, is nothing to shrug off. Ice climbing, ice fishing, snowmobiling, cross-country skiing to a mountain chalet—it's all here. Plus, Aspen is one of the only resort towns in North America with four separate ski mountains and 5,285 acres of terrain, all of it world-class. But the Highland Bowl—on Aspen Highlands mountain, a free 10-minute shuttle ride away from town—is one of the largest bowls in the world that is entirely "in bounds," meaning that it is maintained by the ski patrol. It had only fully opened in 2002, after I'd last skied Aspen, and I knew this time I would have to take it on.

That night I rode into town. Strung over Main Street was a colorful banner advertising the week's events: the Junior National ski races, a concert by pianist Stephen Hough, a reading by Pulitzer Prize winner Richard Russo, and the public radio fund-raising drive. I hopped out at Galena Street and walked toward the historic Elks Building in the center of town. Window after storefront window gleamed with shiny jewelry and designer clothing: Zegna, Gucci, and Dior, all staking their sidewalk claims. The old Ute City Pub I used to love was now, to my dismay, a Burberry. Still, it was all but impossible to be depressed. Though it had been snowing on and off and the temperature was in the twenties, the dry air was crisp and invigorating, and the scenery in all directions—the mountains, the valley, the cozy lamplit streets—was simply staggering. "You know, just another day in paradise," I overheard a man saying on his cell phone as he passed me, and I found myself nodding hello.

I had dinner plans with an Aspen fixture named Tim Mooney, who had chosen the low-key Topper's Aspen restaurant, a small, warm joint off the beaten path that serves pasta and brick-oven pizzas. When I arrived, he was at a table in back, shaking his head at an item in the *Aspen Daily News* police blotter. (My favorite during my stay: STRANGER FOUND SLEEPING IN ASPEN HOME.)

Mooney had a story like those of many residents I met. He arrived in Aspen in 1970 during a stopover on a road trip and never left. Since then he's had many careers: he was a tour manager for Aspenites John Denver and Jimmy Buffett; he was a ski instructor for 23 years (and served for many of them as Jack Nicholson's private teacher) until he was famously fired in 2001 for chainsawing trees on the mountain to make a new ski trail. In his honor, residents now call the run "The Dark Side of Mooney." In his latest incarnation, Mooney is a real estate broker with Sotheby's, which he admits "isn't the best way to make a living at the moment." But despite the downturn, the average home price in Aspen is $4.3 million; a $40 million spec house is being built on Red Mountain; and at Aspen's sister mountain, Snowmass, a colossal $1.3 billion base development—nearly a million square feet of new condos, houses, commercial spaces, and time-shares—is set to open this year. "The incredible power of this little town," Mooney said, shaking his balding head and putting back a Merlot.

OPPOSITE: A pair of lift operators at Buttermilk.

TOP, FROM LEFT: A reveler at Hotel Jerome; Tasmanian snapper and English-pea risotto at Cloud Nine Alpine Bistro; a snowboarder on Buttermilk. BELOW: Aspen restaurateurs *(from left)* Tommy Tolleson, Denise Walters, and Gunnar Sachs.

WHEN I REACHED THE SUMMIT, THE SKY BEGAN TO CLEAR AND I STOOD GASPING AT THE 360-DEGREE VIEW

"About fifteen hundred people vote in Aspen. In 2008 there were $2.5 billion in real estate transactions."

We talked about how much had changed since the time both of us began coming here more than three decades ago. Back then, about a hundred babies per year were delivered at Aspen Valley Hospital; now the average is more than 300. Growth and development had always dominated local politics, and in that regard, nothing has changed—at least nothing for the better, in Mooney's view. "We used to have a mom-and-pop ski town with old European-style hotels. Now, we have these new parked cruise ships at the base of Aspen Mountain," he said, referring to the luxury hotels that have opened in the past several years. Mooney believes a setback in the battle against overdevelopment was the death in 2005 of long-time Aspen resident and activist Hunter S. Thompson. When Thompson was alive, Mooney and a group of regulars met weekly in Hunter's kitchen at Owl Farm, in what many describe as "the command center of Aspen politics." There they strategized about how to keep out what Thompson called the Greedheads, and limit development. In 1995, for example, the group successfully campaigned to prevent 737's from flying into the airfield—today there are more than 150 commercial flights per week but no 737's—using a now-celebrated campaign poster designed by the late artist Tom Benton with the slogan THERE IS SOME SHIT WE WON'T EAT.

One of the latest fights concerns the expansion of the airport runway. "Hunter would have been

vicious about this," Mooney said. "We lost the most powerful voice there was standing up for the little guy against big business."

While we were eating, his phone rang. It was his friend, painter Paul Pascarella, another Thompson pal, who was coming to town for an exhibition of his work at a leading fine art gallery—one of the dozens in Aspen that feature artists of national repute. "That's the funny thing about this town," Mooney said. "I don't need to go to New York or Los Angeles to find out what's going on. They come to me."

I SPENT THE NEXT SEVERAL DAYS LIVING SO FAR above my means I almost expected to be arrested, which may not have been entirely unfortunate. I was, after all, between apartments, and the Pitkin County Jail, I learned from the riffraff I was carousing with, has beautiful views, great meals, and free painting classes offered by Aspen artists. (One of the town's most recent soap operas was the re-election of sheriff Bob Braudis to his sixth term, never mind that he actually campaigned for a time from an alcohol rehab center.)

I skied the fresh powder on Aspen Mountain, or Ajax, as the locals call it, and had one of the best meals of my life at Montagna, inside the luxurious classic Aspen ski-in, ski-out hotel, the Little Nell (which reopened for the 2009–2010 winter season following an $18 million dollar renovation by interior designer Holly Hunt). There, chef Ryan Hardy, a Southwest finalist for the 2008 James Beard Awards, lists his olive oils on the menu like wine, and cooks up his delicacies with produce and meat—I devoured a juicy lamb sausage with rapini and mustard—from his own nearby organic farm. Another night, I went out to the Richard Russo reading at the Given Institute, a state-of-the-art conference center nestled in the oldest residential neighborhood in Aspen, where many of the homes still have the original Sears-catalog frames. Inside, the lecture-hall setting was formal—"Thank you for inviting me to the UN," Russo joked when he took the podium—but the feel was small-town block party. Ski instructors, restaurant managers, former mayor Helen Klanderud, and others gabbed in the atrium before the event.

Afterward, a big group flocked through the snowy streets to the Victorian house of Lois Smith Brady, frequent author of the popular *New York Times* Vows column. A small, quick-witted blonde with a generous wine pour, Brady wove her guests together, and by the end of the night I

found myself with her, Russo, and several others in the kitchen, all of us but Russo pledging to do the Bowl together later in the week. I tottered back to my hotel and, entertaining notions of missing my return flight for the next several years, decided to take a ride "down valley" the next day, where the area's most rapid development has been taking place.

The ripple effect of Aspen's eminence and high price tag has kicked off the gentrification of formerly low-income, mostly Hispanic towns like Basalt and Carbondale, which today have nearly $1 million average home prices and attract people from all over the country. Aspen residents now head to Carbondale each month for the First Fridays Art Walk, in which the whole downtown is closed for gallery openings and parties pour into the streets. Architect Michael Lipkin had a major impact on the area's development, founding and building a planned community called Willits. Twenty-two miles from Aspen, Willits is a New Urbanist town similar to Florida's Seaside, which was created by classmates of Lipkin's from the Yale School of Architecture. "The concept was to develop a community where everything is within walking distance," said Lipkin, who moved to Aspen from Manhattan in the 1980's.

Willits now has 1,800 residents, and represents a brand of sane and sustainable development. There's a lake, soccer fields, and a running path winding through a long park. At its end is a traditional gridded "downtown"—complete with a wine shop, a dance and yoga studio, and a general store serving gourmet sandwiches and sporting on its brick façade a fading painted replica of an award-winning Conoco ad from the 1950's. Above a strip of restaurants sit two floors of New York–style loft apartments with million-dollar mountain views.

I would have stayed, but I had dinner plans back in Aspen at a restaurant called Social, located in the same downtown building as long-standing Aspen favorite Elevation. Social is also owned by the Elevation team, which includes Gunnar Sachs, son of legendary international playboy Gunter Sachs. A sleek lounge with banquettes, silver globe chandeliers, and a floor-to-ceiling wine rack sitting behind a glass wall,

Social serves tapas-style plates—the Kobe meatballs, Boursin-cheese mashers, and caramelized-onion *jus* were just the ticket for me. Social's affable manager and co-owner Denise Walters—a wicked snowboarder who just completed her third move to Aspen, this time from New York—then took me downstairs to Elevation, where we continued to eat, and drank an *açai* martini that's so delicious the bartender has to hide the Brazilian nectar because the staff keeps sneaking off with it.

All around us, people were talking about where to go next. Some were heading to the bar at Matsuhisa, the Nobu restaurant owned by billionaire Aspen resident Michael Goldberg. I'd been hearing about Goldberg's music club, Belly Up Aspen—the town's first contemporary-music dance venue, which brings in world-class acts (Aimee Mann, Seal, Todd Rundgren) year-round. Just then my phone rang. It was Mooney, who was

having a drink a few blocks away at Pacifica Seafood & Raw Bar. When we got there, the painter Pascarella, a bearded man with a knowing smile, was being toasted on the occasion of his gallery opening. More martinis were had until someone at the bar, recognizing Mooney, came over and offered us tickets to the show at Belly Up. Minutes later we were there, thumping along to the strobe lights and electronic music. In the corner above the dance floor, tucked into the back of the booth, was Goldberg himself, a giant of a man (his brother is the hulking pro wrestler known simply as Goldberg), surrounded by beautiful women.

The place was still rocking around midnight, but I had to be up in a few hours. I was going to meet Mac Smith, the head of the Aspen Highlands Ski Patrol.

THE SKY WAS DARK WHEN MY ALARM WENT off. I checked my e-mail to find that Lois Smith

Ski-patrol chief Mac Smith in his Aspen Highlands office, above. OPPOSITE: Aspen Highlands' Cloud Nine Alpine Bistro.

Brady and the others who had promised to join me on the Bowl had canceled. I dressed and stumbled into the Highlands shuttle. The streets were almost empty, the lights from the Sno-Cats the only visible movement on the mountain. I made my way to the bowels of the Highland base building, following the smell of coffee to the patrol conference room. About 20 people—varying in age from their twenties to fifties, all but three of them men—were gathered around, buckling their ski boots and eating muffins. These were the elite of Aspen, the chosen few who survived Mac Smith's infamous boot camp and were then selected for the most highly regarded patrol in Colorado.

Smith has a huge gray walrus mustache and long eyebrows, one of which turns up and the other down. At exactly 7:55 a.m., he strode into the room with a long lope and leaned against the back wall. Soft-spoken but businesslike, he jumped straight into a rundown of fences and signs to mend, and a follow-up report on a "lost missing person yesterday," who was found and then somehow lost again. Then he turned it over to his staff snow-and-weather expert, a barefoot, gnomelike man with a ZZ Top beard and taped toes, who spoke for nearly half an hour about trade winds and pressure systems, then finished by saying, "That's about all I have."

"Okay, let's go," Smith said, and within a minute the room was empty.

I rode up the lift with Smith, a native of Basalt, who was monitoring the radio strapped around his chest the whole way. When I asked him about the history of the Highland Bowl, he surprised me by getting emotional. He tried to open it first in 1984, but three of his patrolmen were killed while purposely triggering an avalanche. It took him four years to get back the strength to attempt the challenge again. On the day the Bowl opened, he laid three wreaths for his friends. "It's kind of like a dream you don't know will ever come true," he said. There have been no deaths since.

When we got to the top, we skate-skied over to the patrol station, a solar-powered cabin hovering on wooden stilts. Soon a drill was being organized

to train two black Labrador "dog techs" to rescue avalanche victims. With a devious smile, Smith suggested I volunteer to get in "the hole," to which I first agreed, then changed my mind after seeing the tiny chamber six feet under I was going to be buried in. While Smith laughed, I took up a shovel and helped bury two rookie patrolmen. The dogs had never been tested before on the mountain, but within a minute of being set loose, they had located by scent both sites, and stood barking above them.

Finally, it was time to do the Bowl. I put on my helmet and goggles, and strapped my skis onto my back. "Good luck," Smith said, as I headed to the Sno-Cat that would take me up the first third of a mile of the two-mile hike.

THE SKY WAS JUST BEGINNING TO CLOUD over as I got off the cat and began my ascent. Within 20 minutes, there was no trace of life around me. My world had been reduced to wind. I remembered how Smith had told me he'd used more than 10 times the amount of dynamite to control the snow this year than he ever had. I'd also been told how Aspen resident Neal Biedelman, a world-renowned mountaineer who survived Everest with Jon Krakauer, had nearly been buried alive earlier in the season while skiing out of bounds. (For the record, Aspen would finish this particular season with 510 inches of snow; the average per year is 300. Also, for the first time in history, it would open for an encore day of skiing in June.) *That's it,* I thought as I stepped blindly into thin air, *this is my Everest.*

Then I heard a noise. Someone was coming up behind me. I looked over my shoulder to see Semple. "Right on," he said, giving me a thumbs-up and hoofing by. Even as he disappeared into the cloud ahead, I knew then that I'd be okay. When I reached the summit, the sky began to clear and I stood gasping at the 360-degree view. At last one thing was wonderfully clear: as disparate as the interests and impressions that define Aspen are, the staggering physical beauty of the place was the reason they existed at all. Minutes later, I was knee-deep in champagne powder and falling once again for the town I knew and loved.

OPPOSITE: Aspen in the evening, as seen from Red Mountain.

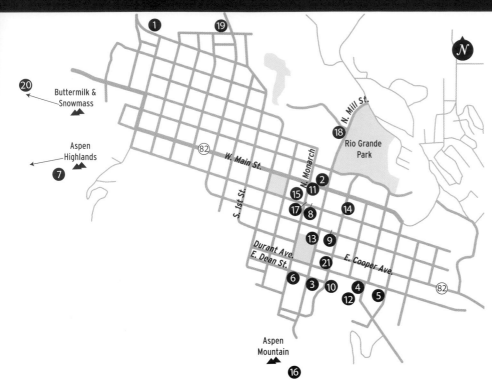

WHEN TO GO
Aspen is a year-round destination, with superb hiking and mountain biking in summer. Ski season runs from Thanksgiving through April. You'll find maximum powder (15 inches per week on average) between January and March. The best deals can be found in November and April.

GETTING THERE + AROUND
The closest airport, serviced by Frontier, United, and Delta Air Lines, is Aspen/Pitkin County Airport. American Airlines and US Airways fly to both Eagle County Regional Airport and Grand Junction Regional Airport. In Aspen, the Roaring Fork Transportation Authority (970/925-8484; rfta.com) runs complimentary shuttles between the mountains.

WHERE TO STAY
1. Aspen Meadows Resort Sprawling hotel compound that also serves as home to the prestigious Aspen Institute. *845 Meadows Rd.; 800/452-4240; dolce-aspen-hotel.com; doubles from $$.*

2. Hotel Jerome, A RockResort European-style grande dame from Colorado's silver-boom days. *330 E. Main St.; 888/367-7625 or 970/920-1000; rock resorts.com; doubles from $$$.*

3. Hyatt Grand Aspen Expansive condominium property a block away from the slopes. *415 E. Dean St.; 800/233-1234 or 970/429-9100; hyatt.com; doubles from $$.*

4. Little Nell Iconic luxury hotel at the base of Aspen Mountain. *675 E. Durant Ave.; 888/843-6355 or 970/920-4600; thelittle nell.com; doubles from $$$$.*

5. Sky Hotel See-and-be-seen slopeside hot spot. *709 E. Durant Ave.; 800/882-2582 or 970/925-6760; theskyhotel.com; doubles from $$$.*

6. St. Regis Aspen Resort Elegant accommodations in the heart of town. *315 E. Dean St.; 877/787-3447 or 970/920-3300; stregis.com; doubles from $$$$.*

WHERE TO EAT + DRINK
Make like a true Aspen insider and partake of the secret, steeply discounted bar menus at fine-dining establishments.

7. Cloud Nine Alpine Bistro Mountain cabin on Aspen Highlands serving wild game and fresh fish. *970/923-8715; lunch for two* ✖✖.

8. Elevation Local favorite serving American fare and açaí martinis. *304 E. Hopkins Ave.; 970/544-5166; dinner for two* ✖✖✖.

9. Ellina Regional ingredients and Slow Food–inspired dishes. *430 E. Hyman Ave.; 970/925-2976; dinner for two* ✖✖✖.

10. Il Mulino New York Outpost of the iconic Manhattan restaurant. *501 E. Dean St.; 970/205-1000; dinner for two* ✖✖✖.

11. Matsuhisa Aspen Another branch of Nobu Matsuhisa's sushi empire. *303 E. Main St.; 970/544-6628; dinner for two* ✖✖✖✖.

12. Montagna At the Little Nell, artisanal cuisine that uses ingredients from the chef's own organic farm. *675 E. Durant Ave.; 970/920-6330; dinner for two* ✖✖✖.

13. Pacifica Seafood & Raw Bar Lively restaurant with a top-notch raw bar. *307 S. Mill St.; 970/920-9775; dinner for two* ✖✖✖.

14. Regal Watering Hole of Aspen Pricey cocktails and a dance floor. *220 S. Galena St.; 720/275-3876; drinks for two* ✖.

Elk osso buco at Cloud Nine Alpine Bistro.

15. Social Scene-setter on Aspen's restaurant row. *304 E. Hopkins Ave.; 970/925-9700; dinner for two* XXX.

16. Sundeck Restaurant On Aspen Mountain, fresh sandwiches and panoramic views. *970/544-9345; lunch for two* XX.

17. Syzygy Restaurant Weekend DJ's, deftly prepared New American dishes, and a first-rate wine list. *308 E. Hopkins Ave.; 970/925-3700; dinner for two* XXX.

18. Topper's Aspen Indulgent eatery featuring delectable soups and pulled-pork sandwiches. *211A Puppy Smith St.; 970/920-0069; dinner for two* XX.

WHAT TO SEE + DO

19. Aspen Institute International nonprofit that hosts seminars, conferences, and other events. *1000 N. Third St.; 970/925-7010; aspeninstitute.org.*

20. Aspen Santa Fe Ballet Nationally recognized company for contemporary dance. *Aspen District Theater; 970/925-7175; aspensantafeballet.com.*

21. Belly Up Aspen Premiere concert venue, showcasing acts from B. B. King to ZZ Top. *450 S. Galena St.; 970/544-9800; bellyupaspen.com.*

OUTFITTERS

Ski & Snowboard School Lessons for every level, plus specialty programs and clinics. *877/282-7736; aspensnowmass.com; lessons from $119 a day.*

Ski Equipment Rental Good source for gear, from boards to bindings. *800/525-6200; aspensnowmass.com; rentals from $32 a day.*

Suit Yourself Mobile Skiwear Rental On-call service that provides all the warm gear you might not have packed. *970/920-0295; from $55 a day.*

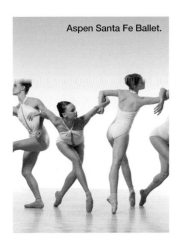

Aspen Santa Fe Ballet.

WHERE TO SKI

Comprehensive information on Aspen Highlands, Aspen Mountain, Buttermilk, and Snowmass, including package deals and lift tickets, can be found at aspensnowmass.com.

Aspen Highlands Home to the famed Highland Bowl. *76 Boomerang Rd.; 800/525-6200.*

Aspen Mountain The first of Aspen's four mountains, and its most centrally located. *601 E. Dean St.; 800/525-6200.*

Buttermilk Wider trails and gentle powder for beginner skiers. *38700 Hwy. 82; 800/525-6200.*

Snowmass The largest of Aspen/Snowmass's four mountains; site of a buzzworthy new base village. *45 Village Square; 800/525-6200.*

FESTIVALS + EVENTS

Aspen Arts Festival More than 170 exhibitors with works from jewelry to painting. *970/925-1940; aspenchamber.org.*

Aspen Ideas Festival Global leaders discuss and debate the defining issues of our time. *970/544-7916; aifestival.org.*

Aspen Music Festival Classical music in a sublime setting.

970/925-3254; aspenmusicfestival.com.

Aspen Summer Words Five-day event and writers' retreat drawing the literary world's top talent. *970/925-3122; aspenwriters.org.*

Boogie's Bash Fourth of July gala and five-mile race supporting Aspen's youth. *970/920-2130; buddyprogram.org.*

ESPN Winter X Games From snowboarding to snowmobiling, this is the annual equivalent of the Winter Olympics for extreme sports. *800/525-6200; aspensnowmass.com.*

First Fridays Art Walk Monthly gallery openings and parties in the nearby town of Carbondale. *Main St., Carbondale; 970/963-1680; carbondale.com.*

***Food & Wine* Classic in Aspen** Cooking demonstrations and tastings against a spectacular backdrop. *970/925-1940; aspenchamber.org.*

Jazz Aspen Snowmass World-class jazz in an intimate outdoor setting. *970/920-4996; jazzaspen.org.*

Wintersköl Four-day festival that includes a soup competition between area chefs. *970/925-1940; aspenchamber.org.*

Aspen Highlands.

LOCAL TIPS

Blazing Trails
Aspen legend Lorenzo Semple III (of Suit Yourself Mobile Skiwear Rental) shares his favorite places to find powder.

Hanging Valley Wall, Snowmass
Descend through glades, chutes, and gullies for extreme-skiing thrills.

Highlands Bowl, Aspen Highlands
Not for the faint of heart, this natural amphitheater gives new meaning to the term *steep and deep.*

Long Shot, Snowmass
Meandering intermediate trail with a secluded, backcountry feel.

1A Lift Line, Aspen Mountain Double-black-diamond run that drops off into town.

Racer's Edge, Buttermilk Popular among speed freaks, who often overlook the pillowy snow clinging to the trail's tree-flanked boundary.

KEY TO THE DINING PRICE ICONS   X UNDER $25   XX $25–$74   XXX $75–$149   XXXX $150–$299   XXXXX $300 AND UP

A guest room at
the Postcard Inn,
in St. Pete Beach,
Florida.

The lobby at
the Royal Hawaiian,
on Oahu.

A view of the atrium
at 21c Museum
Hotel, in Louisville,
Kentucky.

Staffer Mike Doud
at the Resort at Paws
Up, in Greenough,
Montana.

PLACES TO STAY

BOHEMIAN BEACH HOTEL

STAYING TRUE TO ITS SURFER-COOL, 1950'S-MOTEL ROOTS, THE POSTCARD INN, IN ST. PETE BEACH, FLORIDA, IS CAREFREE, HIP, AND RESOLUTELY AFFORDABLE. BY CHARLES GANDEE

Photographed by Blasius Erlinger

UNLIKE FORT LAUDERDALE BEACH AND MIAMI BEACH, TWO OF THE HOTTER SPOTS

on the southeast coast of Florida, St. Pete Beach—on the central west coast of the Sunshine State—is lazy and low-key, quiet and calm, unpretentious and unassuming. More old Florida than new, it has no throngs of party-down revelers looking for a noisy good time in anything-goes clubs with velvet-roped VIP rooms. You will see fewer Porsches and Escalades here cruising Gulf Boulevard, the main thoroughfare dividing the east side of St. Pete Beach from the west; fewer cigar-smoking "players" in Gucci shirts and Prada loafers noisily ordering magnums of Cristal. Instead, you will see a vast array of casual restaurants, plus a full complement of Laundromats, souvenir shops, convenience stores, gas stations, bicycle shops, and surf shacks. If St. Pete Beach has a dress code, it is cutoffs and flip-flops, bathing suits and bare feet.

Here, on this particular stretch of the west coast of Florida, between tiny Pass-A-Grille Beach to the south and Treasure Island to the north, the landscape comprises mostly nondescript two- and three-story motels with colorful neon signs erected in the late 1950's and 60's and then, by the look of things, pretty much left to entropy. One of them, however, has just been renovated and renamed: Postcard Inn on the Beach, an easygoing hotel with a bohemian edge. Built in 1957 as the Colonial Gateway Inn, a 204-room, two-story, U-shaped motel with a large pool and a grove of mature royal palms at its core, it became a Travelodge in 1999. In its latest incarnation, the property joins a wave of stylish, affordable beach hotels, including the Surf Lodge, in Montauk, New York, and the Canary Hotel, in Santa Barbara, California.

The Postcard Inn story begins in 2005, when Barry Sternlicht, the high-profile chairman and CEO of Starwood Capital Group, led his company to acquire the Travelodge, with plans to raze the

motel and build a condo-hotel. But the neighbors banded together and objected to the proposed development, and the plan languished until the economy finally undermined the viability of Sternlicht's project. So he came up with an alternative: renovate the Travelodge to transform what was a down-at-the-heels motel into a chic inn. For that he turned to his friend and business partner Stephen Hanson, founder of B.R. Guest Restaurants, co-owned by Starwood Capital Group.

What Hanson had in mind for St. Pete Beach was not a boutique hotel. The Postcard Inn is a world away from, say, South Beach's Delano and Shore Club. It has neither the aesthetic panache, the too-cool-for-school attitude, nor the room rates of such hotels. Hanson had a dramatically different agenda. "Howard Johnson meets JetBlue is probably where we want to be," he says. In practical terms, he was determined to renovate the aging motel into accessible, affordable accommodations with user-friendly flair. "We're looking to build a successful brand with unique character that will cater to all types of travelers—singles, couples, families with children—looking for more than just the trendiest new hotel," Hanson says.

Collaborating with Hanson on programming, planning, and design was Tara Oxley, head of B.R. Guest Restaurants' in-house design team; Chris Sheffield, principal of Philadelphia-based S.L. Design; and marketing maven Donna Rodriguez, who has worked with Hanson for 16 years. Landscape architect Christy Ten Eyck, based in Phoenix and Austin, Texas, assumed responsibility for everything green.

To focus the team's vision for the hotel, Oxley assembled a bulging scrapbook of images and thoughts that served as inspiration and guide. On

the first page of the book are the words *vintage, American, hot, beachy,* and *getaway*; on the second is a passage from Jack Kerouac about the glory of living life to the fullest. Taped to the following pages is a range of colorful fabric swatches and alluring vignettes, plus evocative snapshots meant to capture the general mood: from seagulls on the sand in the morning and octogenarians taking in the sun on a bench in the afternoon to picture-perfect waves crashing against the Gulf shore.

Though not as popular as Cocoa Beach, on the east coast of Florida, St. Pete Beach boasts a healthy subculture of surfers, who tend to congregate at the nearby Sunset and Upham beaches or, a bit farther north, at the Redington Beach pier. "As an inspirational anchor for Postcard Inn, there is no more authentically American beach tradition than surfing," Rodriguez says. "We really wanted to create a hotel that feels comfortable for the time and natural in its surroundings."

"Lively, easy, up-spirited," adds Hanson, who came to the project with three intractable mandates: "It had to be fun, it had to be affordable, and it had to have the spirit of the locality." To amplify the

last point, he adds, "I think St. Pete Beach is a little treasure, it's an affordable, fun town, and it's two and a half hours from New York. We wanted to be part of the community, part of the local scene."

Toward that end, the guest rooms were to be "reminiscent of surfers' digs," according to the Postcard Inn design team. Driving the idea home, 165 of the rooms come with a bona fide surfboard in the corner (and prudently anchored to the wall).

Because they were committed to an affordable room rate, gutting the period bathrooms was not in the budget. They did, however, do away with all of the kitchenettes, which had been located in several of the rooms; in their place are upholstered, built-in banquettes backed by bamboo paneling and cordoned off with hanging, wood-and-glass-beaded curtains.

Though no two are exactly alike, the rooms all have vintage table lamps on new pickled and stained birch desks, flat-screen TV's, Wi-Fi, and, flanking the beds, classic black-metal drafting lamps with articulated arms. The objective was to jettison the dark, dated, oppressive feel of the Travelodge guest rooms, so they opted for white wood venetian blinds for the windows and a sand-colored, sisal-like

Relaxing in the Postcard Inn's lobby, above left. RIGHT: The hotel entrance. PREVIOUS SPREAD, FROM LEFT: A surf-inspired guest room; the lobby library.

flooring that is actually woven vinyl. Down-filled duvets with crisp white covers have replaced the bedspreads. On the wall behind the beds is either a floor-to-ceiling, wall-to-wall photo mural of a lone surfer on a longboard in the curl of a tsunami-scale wave, a photographic collage of all things surfing-oriented, or a colorful, typographically lively series of quotes from legendary surfers, as well as Thoreau, the Beach Boys, Andy Warhol, Jay-Z, and others.

Between the pool and the beach is the freestanding PCI Beach Bar, formerly called Swigwam, and an adjacent Snack Shack where you can treat yourself to a hamburger. On certain nights of the week, live music adds a festive element to the watering hole, which has been popular with locals since the 1970's. Boccie, shuffleboard, horseshoes, volleyball, and Ping Pong provide diversions, along with tire swings and a basketball hoop. There are also two beachside gyms in two 2-story pavilions: one for cardio, one for weights.

Though there is no room service, a free hot-and-cold continental breakfast is served in a tented "canteen" off the lobby, near a vintage photo booth and a video-game arcade. In a stylistic reprieve

from the surfing/beach motif, the hotel's restaurant, adjacent to the lobby, is a 200-seat offshoot of Hanson's bustling Wildwood BBQ on Park Avenue South, in Manhattan.

Out along Gulf Boulevard, Postcard Inn's exterior signals the refurbished motel within by manipulating the A-line façade, breaking down the monolithic masonry with cypress-wood panels that extend some 40 feet from the corners of the 1957 building toward its center. Cypress panels were also applied to the porte cochère that marks the main entrance to the hotel's lobby, and planters were filled with vines and flowers. "In general," Sheffield says, "we wanted to soften the existing building and introduce a sense of tropical greenery that is indicative of the planting materials and green spaces within the courtyard."

Hanson is convinced that he is on the right track. "Always affordable," he says, when asked about potential projects. And then he adds, "Instead of trying to build three- or four- or five-star hotels for your ego, stay exactly where the market wants to be." The Postcard Inn on the Beach is right on target.

ABOVE, FROM LEFT: The Postcard Inn's PCI Beach Bar; fish tacos at the hotel's Wildwood BBQ & Burger. OPPOSITE: Hitting the beach.

Blackened mahimahi with shrimp at Wildwood BBQ & Burger.

WHEN TO GO

St. Pete Beach is a year-round destination with warmer water from April to November, but its seaside weather is best during spring and early fall, when humidity is at bay. Beware of the occasional tropical storms that can roll through the area in the fall.

GETTING THERE

American Airlines, Delta, and JetBlue have regular flights to Tampa International Airport. From there, St. Pete Beach is a half-hour drive southwest on I-275.

WHERE TO EAT

2. Ceviche Tapas Bar & Restaurant More than 100 small dishes—smoked mussels; rare aged cheeses; chorizo flambéed in Spanish brandy—and weekly flamenco shows in the cavernous basement bar. *10 Beach Dr., St. Petersburg; 727/209-2302; tapas for two* ✗✗.

3. Hurricane Seafood Restaurant Popular family joint that specializes in down-home favorites like breaded gator bites and fresh grouper po'boys. Head to the bars on the rooftop deck for sunset views over the water. *807 Gulf Way; 727/360-9558; dinner for two* ✗✗.

4. Ted Peters Famous Smoked Fish This open-air seafood shack has been a local institution since the 1950's; folks line up for plates of oak-smoked mullet, salmon, and mackerel, or they bring their own catches to toss into the smokehouse. *1350 Pasadena Ave., South Pasadena; 727/381-7931; lunch for two* ✗.

5. Wildwood BBQ & Burger Revered pit master "Big Lou" Elrose mans the outdoor barbecue, which turns out Carolina pulled pork, hand-carved brisket, and baby back ribs served three ways. *Postcard Inn on the Beach, 6300 Gulf Blvd.; 727/369-4950; dinner for two* ✗✗.

WHERE TO SHOP

6. Evander Preston's The larger-than-life artist displays his own distinctive contemporary jewelry and other one-of-a-kind designs in this boutique, which is decorated with African masks, red vinyl booths, and bison-skin rugs. *106 Eighth Ave.; 800/586-3826 or 727/367-7894; evanderpreston.com.*

7. Florida Craftsmen Gallery The state's nonprofit craftsmen's association has a retail store where local artists can sell their creations. *501 Central Ave., St. Petersburg; 727/821-7391; floridacraftsmen.net.*

8. Gas Plant Antique Arcade Four-floor mecca chock-full of dealers. *1246 Central Ave., St. Petersburg; 727/895-0368; gasplantantiquearcade.com.*

9. Haslam's Book Store A 300,000-tome literary haven run by third-generation booksellers.

The Postcard Inn's revamped exterior.

WHERE TO STAY

1. Postcard Inn on the Beach Former motel transformed into a casual-chic seaside retreat. *6300 Gulf Blvd.; 800/237-8918; postcardinn.com; doubles from $.*

The beach at Fort De Soto Park.

2025 Central Ave., St. Petersburg; 727/822-8616; haslams.com.

WHAT TO SEE + DO

10. Fort De Soto Park
Consistently top-rated for its wide white-sand beaches, this 1,100-acre county park also has two fishing piers, six miles of walking and biking trails, and a historic fort dating to the Spanish-American War. *3500 Pinellas Bayway S., Tierra Verde; 727/582-2267; pinellascounty.org.*

11. Salvador Dalí Museum
The permanent collection comprises more than 2,000 of the Surrealist master's oil paintings, sculptures, and objets d'art; a new $36 million facility is planned for early 2011. *1000 Third St. S., St. Petersburg; 727/823-3767; thedali.org.*

12. Sunset Celebration at Pier 60 Popular, free street festival with live bands, magicians, and crafts booths, held every day at Clearwater Beach (weather permitting). *Pier 60, Clearwater Beach; 727/449-1036; sunsetsatpier60.com.*

13. Weedon Island Preserve
A low-lying peninsula surrounded by small islands off northern St. Petersburg, with four miles of canoeing trails (which weave through mangroves and seagrass flats), Native American burial mounds, and a cultural and natural history center offering guided excursions. *1800 Weedon Dr., St. Petersburg; 727/453-6500; weedonislandpreserve.org.*

LOCAL TIPS

The No-Fuss Vacation
Postcard Inn on the Beach developer Stephen Hanson shares his favorite laid-back activities.

14. SIMPLE EATS
"It's really hard to get me away from our property, but when I do leave, I head to local restaurants like the **Waffle House** *(7070 Gulf Blvd.; 727/360-6959; breakfast for two* ✘*)* or have a picnic in nearby Fort De Soto Park."

15. DAY OF PLAY
"When the entire family is in tow, we head to **Busch Gardens** *(10165 N. McKinley Dr., Tampa Bay; 888/800-5447; buschgardens. com)*. It's only a forty-five-minute drive from Postcard Inn, which makes it ideal when we want to take a break from the beach."

16. VINTAGE FINDS
"On the occasional rainy weekend, we like to go antiquing at the **Wagon Wheel Flea Market** *(7801 Park Blvd., Pinellas Park; 727/544-5319)*."

FOUR MORE BEACHFRONT ESCAPES

NEW YORK
Allegria Hotel & Spa
Located 40 minutes outside Manhattan, with 143 rooms, a new Joseph Christopher spa, and the popular, seafood-focused Atlantica restaurant, run by well-regarded Long Island chef Todd Jacobs. *80 W. Broadway, Long Beach; 888/662-3224; allegriahotel. com; doubles from $$.*

NEW YORK
Surf Lodge Helmed by three New York City nightlife impresarios; the breezy, low-key interiors—rattan basket chairs; ocean-inspired artwork—join a haute beachwear boutique and *Top Chef* star Sam Talbot's buzzy restaurant. *183 Edgemere St., Montauk; 631/668-1962; thesurflodge.com; doubles from $$.*

CALIFORNIA
Canary Hotel Just off Santa Barbara's restaurant- and boutique-laden State Street, this 97-room property has Moroccan-style textiles on the walls, interiors inspired by the Canary Islands, and views of the Santa Ynez Mountains. *31 W. Carrillo St., Santa Barbara; 805/884-0300; canary santabarbara.com; doubles from $$.*

CALIFORNIA
Malibu Beach Inn One of the only places to stay in this notoriously exclusive enclave (the so-called "Billionaire's Beach"); a multimillion-dollar refurbishment, courtesy of David Geffen, was completed in October 2007. *22878 Pacific Coast Hwy., Malibu; 310/456-6444; malibubeachinn.com; doubles from $$.*

VIEWING ROOMS

SHOCKING PHOTOGRAPHS IN THE RESTAURANT, CHUCK CLOSE TAPESTRIES IN THE BEDROOMS, RED PLASTIC PENGUINS THROUGHOUT THE PUBLIC SPACES: IN LOUISVILLE, KENTUCKY, THE ECLECTIC 21C ELEVATES *ART HOTEL* TO AN ART FORM. BY RAUL BARRENECHE

IT'S A CRISP EARLY-SPRING SATURDAY IN Kentucky, and I'm having breakfast with New York City architect Deborah Berke and one of her clients, the philanthropist, art collector, and hotelier Steve Wilson. We're in Wilson's art-filled 19th-century Georgian mansion on Woodland Farm, a 1,000-acre estate overlooking the Ohio River outside Louisville where Wilson lives with his wife, Laura Lee Brown, a member of the clan that controls the $2.7 billion liquor conglomerate Brown-Forman. (The company began distilling bourbon in 1870 and now owns Jack Daniels, Southern Comfort, Finlandia vodka, and Fetzer wines, among others.) There's art everywhere—painting, photography, video, sculpture—all of it contemporary, much of it provocative. But the house looks relatively bare, Berke remarks. Indeed, between the life-size black-and-white image of a 1970's male porn star, meticulously rendered with hundreds of tiny stamens from plastic flowers, and the stacked vitrines displaying dozens of anatomically detailed phallic champagne flutes ("We used these on New

Year's Eve," Wilson says, with a laugh), I notice holes in the walls, and empty hooks and hangers. Wilson confirms that they've moved many canvases and photographs to their 21c Museum Hotel, in downtown Louisville. The 90-room property, which occupies five 19th-century brick buildings on West Main Street, is Wilson and Brown's passion, and represents one of the most ambitious unions of art and hospitality ever undertaken.

The term *museum hotel* says everything about Wilson and Brown's mission. They see 21c as a bona fide cultural institution in the making, not just a hotel with art. Hiring Berke, a thoughtful minimalist and Yale professor who designed Industria Superstudios, in New York City, and the Yale School of Art, in New Haven, adds gravitas to the endeavor. Nearly three-quarters of the paintings, sculptures, photos, and video installations at 21c are part of Wilson and Brown's personal collection, valued at an undisclosed sum of millions. In addition, the International Contemporary Art Foundation (ICAF) commissions

OPPOSITE: A guest room with Pierre Gonnord's *Nico,* at 21c Museum Hotel.

site-specific installations to fill the hallways, restaurant, bar, and 9,000 square feet of exhibition space. All of the works on view were produced by living artists—hence the hotel's name, a reference to the 21st century.

Wilson and Brown have hired a full-time museum director and lined up guest curators to organize twice-yearly temporary exhibitions as

ART HAS BECOME A HOTEL AMENITY IN AMERICA, ONE THAT PROVIDES GUESTS WITH GLIMPSES OF BEAUTY OR THE SHOCK OF THE NEW

well as multiple smaller shows. These shows draw primarily on ICAF's holdings, but also display work from other collections and institutions. The inaugural exhibition, "Hybridity: The Evolution of Species and Spaces in 21st-Century Art," included three wallpaper-like prints by American artist Nicolas Lampert on loan from MASS MoCA. Wilson says future shows will focus on themes such as fame, vanity, and death.

However you frame it, art has become a hotel amenity in America, one that bestows upon properties a sheen of sophistication and provides guests with glimpses of beauty or the shock of the new. At the Gramercy Park Hotel, in New York, art patron Aby Rosen collaborated with Ian Schrager to bring in works that include pieces by Andy Warhol, Keith Haring, and Jean-Michel Basquiat. Another Warhol is on hand at the Joule, in Dallas, owned by oilman Tim Headington. Hotel chains are building corporate collections to showcase in the lobbies and guest rooms of their properties. Sonesta's 7,000 works, by Frank Stella, Sol LeWitt, Roy Lichtenstein, and others, are spread among the company's mid-market hotels and resorts; guests can get printed guides at the four U.S. properties of the art on site. The Four Seasons Hotel at East Palo Alto attempts to wow tech moguls with paintings and sculptures by Miró and Dalí. At the Park Hyatt Chicago, you can find works by Isamu Noguchi and

Dale Chihuly. The focal point of the lobby is Gerhard Richter's *Piazza del Duomo, Milan*, a 27-foot canvas that was purchased from Sotheby's for a reported $3.6 million.

Hotels that are smaller and style-conscious tend to prefer contemporary work to mainstream masterpieces, not only for their less prohibitive price tags but also for the awe factor. The Sagamore, in South Beach, a favorite with the Art Basel crowd, has been assembling a collection of Walker Evanses, Carlos Betancourts, and Liza May Posts, curated by Christine Taplin. Le Méridien Chambers Minneapolis showcases works by Tracey Emin, Damien Hirst, and other contemporary artists. Even hotels without the means to acquire blue-chip art are tapping into this trend. Kimpton's Alexis Hotel, in Seattle, mounts quarterly exhibitions of Pacific Northwest works in its own on-site Art Walk.

By the standards of Louisville, where overnight options have been limited to the stuffy Seelbach and Brown hotels or a corporate chain, 21c is off the charts. My room is actually a corner suite on the second floor, with 12-foot-high ceilings, arched windows, and views of the well-preserved cast-iron façades of the old distilleries along Main Street, once known as Whiskey Row. Many of the hotel's rooms face a glassed-in atrium above the basement-level gallery. Much of the artwork is labeled, but Wilson says he's also planning to publish a catalogue of information accessible by smart phone. I learn that the photos above my bed are by French artist Pierre Gonnord and that the small images behind the dining table are by Loretta Lux. A tapestry that I instantly recognize as a pixelated work by Chuck Close hangs between two of the windows. Viewed from an angle, it comes into focus as a portrait of the photographer Lucas Samaras.

Berke's firm custom-designed many furniture pieces, including a stylish table topped with metallic blue glass and a cabinet that conceals two 42-inch plasma TV's—one for viewing from the bed, another for watching from the living area. A sleek black alarm clock has a built-in dock for an iPod, which the staff has loaded with an eclectic mix of music.

OPPOSITE, FROM LEFT: The skylit atrium at 21c, which reveals much of the original 1860's structure; a suite with a portrait by Chuck Close that now hangs in the Atrium Gallery.

Unlike other art-focused hotels, 21c looks beyond the captive audience of overnight guests. Wilson and Brown hope to attract visitors to the city with the art in the hotel's public spaces, making 21c a vital part of downtown Louisville. "We asked ourselves, 'Can art stimulate business and generate economic development?'" Wilson tells me over bison tenderloin and country-ham fritters on a busy Friday night at the hotel's restaurant, Proof on Main. "We wanted to build a major project around art. And we wanted to be part of the revitalization of downtown. So a hotel seemed a natural fit."

FOLLOWING THE BILBAO MODEL, ART AND architecture have become reliable components of urban renewal. In Louisville, where tourist season lasts for a single spring weekend, during the running of the Kentucky Derby, it's long been a challenge to lure people downtown. The appeal of horse country and the beautiful rolling bluegrass hills outside the city is undeniable. Hollywood superproducer Jerry Bruckheimer and his Louisville-born wife, Linda Balahoutis, have a sprawling horse farm 20 miles from the city center. The ruler of Dubai and his family own 5,000 acres in the area and raise prize-winning Thoroughbreds. But in the town itself there are pedestrian-friendly streets and a fantastic collection of 19th-century cast-iron buildings second only to that of New York's SoHo neighborhood. A block from 21c is a 26-story building, headquarters of insurance giant Humana, that was designed by Michael Graves and helped launch the postmodern architecture movement in 1985. All Louisville needs to be a thriving, growing, modern downtown, Wilson figures, is a few anchor attractions.

Perhaps a hotel with two galleries won't turn Louisville into the new Bilbao overnight, but the city is betting that concentrating a handful of cultural options downtown will strengthen its urban heart. Already there are several draws within walking distance of 21c. The Kentucky

Museum of Art & Craft occupies one of the renovated cast-iron buildings across the street. The Louisville Slugger Museum is a couple of doors down, its giant baseball bat leaning against the brick façade. A few blocks east along the riverfront is the Muhammad Ali Center, and a few blocks west of that is the Actors Theater, where the Humana Festival of New American Plays brings in producers and scouts from around the country each spring.

Still, Wilson and Brown are the biggest players in the downtown rejuvenation. The couple paid more than $30 million for the renovation of the hotel buildings. (Historic-preservation tax credits helped offset some of the cost, and the city pitched in a $1.7 million starter grant.) They've joined forces with a local developer to build Museum Plaza, a futuristic 61-story high-rise designed by REX. The $465 million venture will house residential units, offices, a hotel, and a new art museum floating 20 stories above the riverfront. But until that ambitious project is completed, 21c remains the city's star attraction.

On this Friday night, Proof is packed with a buzzing mix of Louisville's young-and-fashionable set and old-guard stalwarts. They eat surrounded by a trio of sinewy goats strung above the open kitchen on ropes (earthenware sculptures by ceramic artist Beth Cavener Stichter), and a wooden stag head wearing a leather S&M mask (a piece by Michael Combs). Most of the crowd seems nonplussed by the art; some wander around the gallery after dinner in wide-eyed bewilderment, not sure what to make of the flock of four-foot-tall red plastic penguins by the Cracking Art Group. (The flock "migrates" throughout the property day and night, with help from the hotel's staff.) "We didn't want the art to dominate the space—you have to be careful not to scare people," Berke says. Staffers tell me that Louisville has good restaurants, but locals aren't used to venturing downtown for dinner. The art should help draw suburbanites to Proof, and the cuisine—much of it from local suppliers and organic farms, including the chef's own—will feed the museum's audience.

Meanwhile, the affable Wilson, a onetime art student and the public-relations man for three former Kentucky governors, is getting a kick out of gauging people's responses to the art ("It's provocative, but not unapproachable"), not to mention the nonstop nightly meeting and greeting. "I've never had so much fun in my entire life," he says. Afterward, as we walk through the galleries, Wilson explains that his taste for art with high shock value comes from his rural Kentucky childhood. "I couldn't wait to get off the farm. Everyone was very conservative and very repressed, especially about sex," he says.

The galleries themselves were designed by Berke in her usual spare-but-polished industrial style. The temporary exhibition space, located where most hotels would put the lobby, has dark-wood floors, exposed-brick walls, and beadboard ceilings that contrast with slender painted-steel columns. A staircase leads down to another gallery, a skylit atrium with polished concrete floors, exposed-brick piers, and steel trusses towering above Yinka Shonibare's *The Sleep of Reason Produces Monster (Europe)*, and other works.

Because the project entailed the restoration of five historic buildings, including the former Bunbury Theater and the old Falls City Tobacco Bank, Berke had to reveal as much of the original 1860's structures as possible. Her team also salvaged old poplar floorboards and joists and turned them into bar fronts, banquettes, and the front desk. The restaurant floors are made from recycled carpet backing; the black headboard walls in the guest rooms are made of panels of tiny black beads that were once milk containers. These elements lend textures to the interiors that suit the historic architecture.

Wilson and Brown are hoping to bring a number of new museum hotels, also designed by Berke, to small cities around the country. They're restoring a historic building in downtown Cincinnati and planning a mixed-use complex in downtown Austin, Texas, as well as scouting other locations. "We want cities with a university and a youthful attitude," Wilson says. "We want to be somewhere that might be starving for art."

OPPOSITE, CLOCKWISE FROM TOP LEFT: The kitchen at Proof on Main, 21c's restaurant; the dining room; an exhibition in the hotel's Atrium Gallery; sculptures by artist Judy Fox in the lobby.

GUIDE TO LOUISVILLE, KENTUCKY

N
Ohio River
64
W. Market St.
2
4
1
W. Main St.
S. 8th St.
S. 7th St.
65
S. Hancock St.
S. Clay St.
S. Shelby St.
3

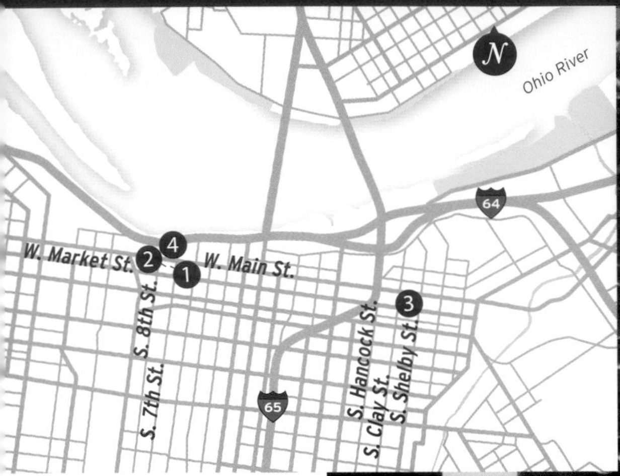

WHERE TO STAY

1. 21c Museum Hotel Owned by a pair of art lovers and philanthropists who mine their personal collection for the property's roster of contemporary works. *700 W. Main St.; 877/217-6400 or 502/217-6300; 21cmuseumhotel.com; doubles from $.*

WHERE TO EAT + DRINK

2. Proof on Main In the art-stocked belly of 21c, a restaurant that melds Italian and local Southern influences. *702 W. Main St.; 502/217-6360; dinner for two XX.*

WHAT TO SEE + DO

3. Green Building Gallery Light-filled space displaying art focused on themes of sustainability. *732 E. Market St.; 502/561-1162; thegreenbuilding.com.*

4. Kentucky Museum of Art & Craft Creative hub with some prime-time-ready names. *715 W. Main St., Louisville; 502/589-0102; kentuckyarts.org.*

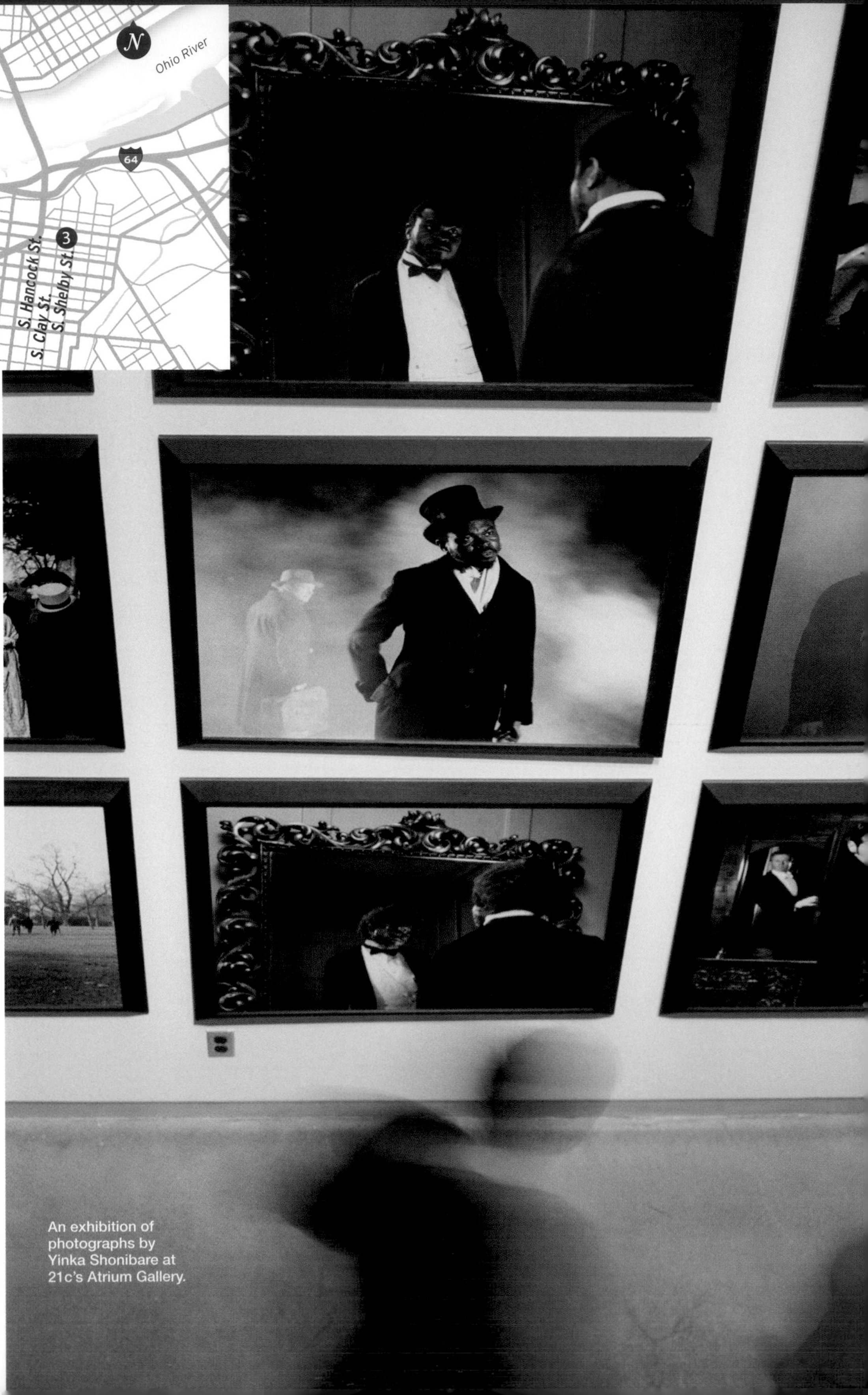

An exhibition of photographs by Yinka Shonibare at 21c's Atrium Gallery.

SIX MORE AMERICAN HOTELS WITH NOTEWORTHY ART COLLECTIONS

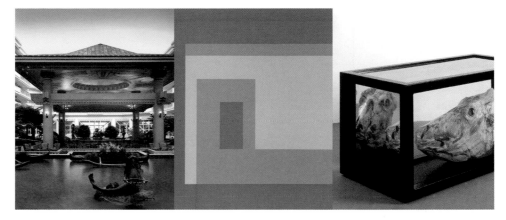

HAWAII
Grand Wailea Maui Features 18 bronze sculptures by Fernand Léger and Jan Fisher's *Mermaid of Wailea (above).* *3850 Alanui Dr., Wailea, Maui; 800/888-6100 or 808/875-1234; grandwailea. com; doubles from $$$.*

CALIFORNIA
Four Seasons Hotel at East Palo Alto One highlight of the collection: Josef Albers's oil on canvas *Formulation: Articulation. 2050 University Ave., East Palo Alto; 800/332-3442 or 650/566-1200; fourseasons.com; doubles from $$.*

MINNESOTA
Le Méridien Chambers Minneapolis Damien Hirst's *Judas Iscariot,* a bull's head suspended in a formaldehyde-filled glass case, is part of the artist's *Twelve Disciples* series. *901 Hennepin Ave., Minneapolis; 800/543-4300 or 612/767-6900; lemeridien.com; doubles from $.*

TEXAS
The Joule, A Starwood Luxury Collection Hotel Art consultant John Runyon, in collaboration with owner Tim Headington, brought in black-and-white photographs by Brian Tihany *(above)* and Andy Warhol's silk-screen print *Electric Chairs. 1530 Main St., Dallas; 888/ 627-7119 or 214/748-1300; the joulehotel.com; doubles from $$.*

ILLINOIS
Park Hyatt Chicago Along with site-specific pieces by well-known Chicago artists Judy Ledgerwood and Mary Brogger, the hotel features Gerhard Richter's 27-foot *Piazza del Duomo, Milan. 800 N. Michigan Ave.; 800/233-1234 or 312/335-1234; park. hyatt.com; doubles from $.*

FLORIDA
The Sagamore The hotel rotates its video installations, including Brian Dewan's filmstrip *Before the White Man,* throughout the lobby, video garden, and a dedicated art lounge. *1671 Collins Ave., Miami Beach; 305/535-8088; sagamorehotel. com; doubles from $$.*

KEY TO THE HOTEL PRICE ICONS $ UNDER $250 $$ $250–$499 $$$ $500–$749 $$$$ $750–$999 $$$$$ $1,000 AND UP
KEY TO THE DINING PRICE ICONS X UNDER $25 XX $25–$74 XXX $75–$149 XXXX $150–$299 XXXXX $300 AND UP

A WINTER'S TALE

BRAVING THE SNOW AND COLD, TAMING
SNOWMOBILES AND HORSES, SIGNING UP FOR
ELABORATE MASSAGES, AND FEASTING ON COMFORT
FOOD, AN INTREPID REPORTER SAVORS THE
QUINTESSENTIAL WINTER LODGE EXPERIENCE IN
MONTANA. BY GARY SHTEYNGART

Photographed by Andrea Fazzari

TWO EASTERNERS—MY GIRLFRIEND E. AND I— ARRIVE AT THE MISSOULA, MONTANA, AIRPORT

to the tableau of a stuffed mountain lion eating a stuffed mountain goat above the baggage carousel. The goat is gasping for its life; the pouncing lion looks insatiable. Meanwhile, a roughly hewn man in a Stetson and duster (many Montanans helpfully reinforce a visitor's image of their state) calls out to another one, "Bill Cowley, you old sea dog! I haven't seen you since the Navy!"

"Cut. That's a wrap," I want to say to the phantom cameraman filming this Coen brothers western.

We have landed somewhere at the edge of the continental United States to experience a high-end, very mediated encounter with nature at a place called the Resort at Paws Up, 40 minutes from Missoula. In the adventuring industry, E. and I are what are called Soft Adventurers. Literally, we are soft. We don't exercise more than necessary to remain alive. We both failed the President's Council on Physical Fitness test under the Reagan administration, an exam that included five difficult activities such as the one-mile run, the right-angle push-up, and the partial curl-up (not partial enough). In a mirror image of the president's fitness test, we have decided to submit ourselves to five winter activities that we would never imagine doing without a professional staff of coddlers: the lunatic sport of snowmobiling, the debilitating art of snowshoeing, riding on top of a horse, shooting things with a gun, and standing ass-deep in a frozen river waiting for the trout to bite. All this will be done underneath Montana's famously big sky, to the accompaniment of excellent food, a Tolstoy-size wine list, and every creature comfort the Soft Adventurer needs to feel loved in the face of nature's cruel indifference. Even E.'s dog, Bill, a feisty Jack Russell terrier with no sense of limits, has come to submit himself to an intensive doggy massage at the hands of a professional.

Yawning from the endless plane ride, we pull up to a Paws Up Big Timber cabin, a nearly 1,500-square-foot spread towering over four private acres of land. The houses are named after fly-fishing flies—the Frog Knobbler, Glimmer Stone, the Bunyan Bug, and our very own Pan Fish Popper, with the hot tub gurgling away on the front porch. Inside, the décor is Ponderosa modern: from the photos of cowboys learning the ropes to the cowhide rugs, couches big enough to seat the cast of *Bonanza*, and the Last Best Bed™ (more on the constant trademarking later), which, like an SUV, can be reached with the aid of a stepladder. Lurking amid this Brobdingnagian setup is a kind of induced homeliness. Nothing has been spared—from the satellite TV to the heated floors in the bathroom to the all-important Wi-Fi signal, which I try to catch with my temperamental iPhone. In advance of tomorrow's snowmobiling adventure, I read the "Wisconsin Snowmobiles Fatality Summary" and several online articles such as "Why Are There So Many Michigan Snowmobile Fatalities?" (yes, pray tell, why?) and "Montana Avalanche Victim Survives an 8-Hour Burial." Throughout the night, I can hear E. quaking and mumbling next to me as she dreams about flying off a mountain. Outside, the deathly darkness of a rural night; inside, two figures twisting and turning across their monstrous, hovering bed with its 300-thread-count linens and badger-size pillows. Only Bill the Dog will know the sleep of the righteous.

DAY 2: IT BEGINS

I have to say I really like the bathroom. The slate walls and glass-box showers are fine, but what sets me at ease is the picture-window view of the resort's ubiquitous ponderosa pines, their roots blanketed by the year's last snow, and over the horizon, the loaded grandeur of a nearby mountain

range. According to Larry Lipson, one of the owners, the bathroom is "big enough to put a horse in." He is not being figurative.

"This could be our last meal together," we tell each other over breakfast before commencing our snowmobile appointment. The morning grub is exceptional: a grilled vanilla huckleberry coffee cake topped with caramelized bananas and finished with preserved huckleberries alongside fresh eggs and slabs of flaky ham.

Over at the Wilderness Outpost Center, a nice young man named Jake Hansen dresses us in warm overcoats and snaps on helmets and safety goggles. Asked what's it like to pilot a snowmobile, he says, "It's somewhere between riding a bike and driving a car." Since I can do neither, I let E. take the first turn at the throttle. "Okay, if you start to tip over," Hansen tells us, "you want to just slide off the vehicle. You don't want to stick your leg out." The sleek machine starts to tremble beneath us. We promptly tip over. I stick my leg out. Several tries later, all four limbs miraculously still attached to my torso, we are slowly rumbling uphill, my safety glasses fogging up with fear as every bump sends us jolting into the frozen air,

our lips coated with fresh snow. We ascend 4,000 feet. As the pines flash past us, I try to focus on the unimpeachable beauty of the mountain range through which we are hurtling, a beauty this environmentally un-kosher machine is probably destroying, but instead the particulars of the snowmobile "Fatality Summary" present themselves. "Victim...went off a steep embankment [like the one just to our left]...and struck several trees." Victim "went airborne 20–30 feet into a [pine?] tree." And taken from another snowmobile advisory website: "*Many* [emphasis mine] cases of decapitation have occurred."

Several hours and a few lorazepam pills later, I start to feel better. I've been in dangerous parts of the world before, have been threatened with large knives and kidnapping, and I've found that sooner or later my body gets tired of the constant exposure to stress and a surprisingly blissful feeling descends. Decapitation? Sure. Anything to relax. We pull into the well-preserved and oddly bucolic Garnet ghost town, a collection of timber cabins that, according to our guide, at the turn of the last century housed 1,000 miners, 13 bars, and one very busy jail. Surrounded by the hypnotically simple architecture and the remnants of our country's over-the-top frontier history, we snack on Paws Up gourmet turkey sandwiches and shiver in the midday cold.

After lunch, it's my turn to drive.

The last time I operated a motor vehicle was as a college sophomore, a cross-country trip that nearly ended when an Oldsmobile I was driving collided with one of Alabama's Shoney's franchises. This time around, after a few errant swipes at a snowbank, I begin to warm to the machine beneath me. It becomes evident that the snowmobile operates on the same principle as the American economy—you've got to rev it up something crazy, or the whole thing will just stall and flip over. Soon we're floating along the mountain ridges within a noxious cloud of gas, beneath us the sharp outlines of an endless constellation of trees, above us a sky so frighteningly clear and blue that it feels like a riff on eternity. And for a brief moment, I allow myself to actually enjoy the ride.

Back in our Big Timber cabin with the CNN blaring and the Wi-Fi pumping, I pick up my copy of the indispensable 1,160-page Montana anthology *The Last Best Place*; along with Big Sky Country, this is one of the state's favorite nicknames. The owners of Paws Up, the Lipson family, have riled the heck out of the state's governor and residents by trying to trademark "The Last Best Place" (they also own the trademarks to "The Last Best Bed" and "The Last Best Beef"). The legal fight hasn't exactly made them popular in these parts, but no matter: we settle into the Last Best Hot Tub (trademark pending?) on our front porch and let the late-winter snow coat our tired faces.

DAY 3: BILL THE DOG GETS A SPECIAL TREAT

The damage from yesterday's snowmobiling adventure: throbbing pain in buttocks (from prolonged tension), throbbing pain in biceps (from nervously gripping throttle, E.'s waist), general back pain (unexplained).

After another superb breakfast, this one of granola-studded griddle cakes and the big fat taste of pork-turkey sausage, we head off for another day of what the promotional material refers to as "Roughing It Redefined.™" The first challenge: snowshoeing. Walking through the half-melted snow, our guide points out sagebrush, wolf lichen,

and the rather graceful pellet-like droppings that deer leave behind. We watch a girl gang of white-tailed deer streaming across the woods. The sight of these fit, glorious creatures and of a red-tailed hawk floating on the wind angers me: Here I am, my feet tied to a piece of ergonomic plastic, and this stunning bird is lifted up into the heavens, his strong wings buffeted by temperate gusts.

It's time for some well-earned Soft Adventurer comfort. Over at the spa center, using hot black river rocks and wet towels, a masseur restores my urban dignity in the face of nature's subtle

A HERD OF ELK FILLS OUR PICTURE WINDOW WITH THEIR ELEGANT PRANCING, TO COMPLETE THE VISTA OF SNOW AND PINE

contempt. In another room, a woman named Andrea Hren is rubbing Bill the Dog along both sides of his furry spine. "I'm getting all the little meaty parts and the thighs," she says as Bill's ears settle back. "Can we get that tail going?" Hren says, but Bill is too sedated to wag, his brown eyes staring placidly ahead, all dreams of chasing black squirrels vanquished, replaced with a deep understanding of some canine-headed god.

We dine at Pomp. The chef does especially well with meat—the bison is full of juice and char—and the wine list offers some fine Pinot Noirs from the Willamette Valley. The appetizer of lobster bisque with a lobster corn dog is sweet and just a little tawdry, like a cheap date in Vegas, where the chef earned his culinary stripes. At Tank, Pomp's adjoining bar, we play chess beneath a moose head, listening to the amiable bartender discuss his favorite part of the mountain lion—the haunches—over an endless stream of Hawaiian music.

DAY 4: LET ME SEE YOUR GAME FACE

The weather doesn't know what it wants to be today: snow, fog, drizzle, teasing bursts of sunshine. We put on hip waders and head down to the Blackfoot River. We learn the terminology: casting upstream, strike indicator, nymph fishing, Georgia Brown Stone fly. We learn to keep our elbows close to our bodies, to "pretend there's a Bible there" and

OPPOSITE, FROM LEFT: Snowmobiling to the ghost town of Garnet; Paws Up's doggy massage.

TOP, FROM LEFT: A Paws Up ranch staffer; tying flies bound for the Blackfoot River; a bison burger with a side of salt-and-vinegar fries. BELOW: One of two bedrooms in the Pan Fish Popper cabin.

the end of our appointed hour, I just want to shoot everything in sight. Slowly but indubitably, Paws Up is making a man out of me.

On the ride back to the resort, the doctor ruffles the thick red mane of his youngest. "I appreciate your good manners, boy," he says. As a newly minted sharpshooter I smile and nod my head, wondering why my New York daddy never says things like that.

DAY 5: THE LAST BEST HORSE

It is time to subdue our final fear. I've never been atop an equine, and E.'s experience with riding involved a runaway horse sprinting down a hill and nearly killing her. With that in mind, the Paws Up staff have provided her with one of the resort's tamest, smartest quarter horses, the amazing Guy. I am given the slightly mediocre Fifty, with his chestnut complexion and propensity to snort at the world around him like some willful teenager.

Not being experienced in these things, I use my dog language: "Good boy, Fifty. Good boy. Who's a good boy? You are!" The animal ignores me, gets distracted by a passing deer, and then charges up a hill like there's not 140 pounds of quivering man atop him. While E.'s Guy carefully gauges the terrain, Fifty and I fall right through the melting snow, the horse's belly grazing the ice. After half an hour of riding the beast I feel somewhat beleaguered. But E. has conquered her fear of horses.

On our last morning, while I'm still reeling from shotgun-recoil chest pain and horse prostate, a herd of elk comes running out, stage left, to fill our bedroom's picture window with their elegant prancing, to complete the vista of snow and pine. Twenty elk does are in the thrall of a young buck, an alpha male who marches them around the clearing in back of our cabin and then whisks them off into the woods.

Outside, we walk past the little county-run one-room schoolhouse where four boys, ages 4 to 12, are taught by one full-time teacher and a teacher's aide. The schoolhouse was there before the Lipsons bought the property, and it now sits oddly amid the luxurious accommodations, with its diminutive red bell tower, kid-size basketball court, and the humble cars of its small staff. That's the final piece of Montana I take back home with me to New York, a city where the sky knows its place, where it broods tiredly over our civilization, and where we pay it no heed.

then not to drop it. We catch nothing. But standing on a rock surrounded by the snowbanked river, feeling its rhythms, the strength of the wind, the sting of ice against your fingers, the little crabs of pain running up and down your casting arms, there's a quiet beauty to the endless repetition. There is the hope that something will come your way, will bite, but in the end you come to accept that you are just a biped in rubber waders standing in the middle of endless creation as snow falls all around you and the fish go their own way.

We eat a rejuvenating lunch of tender buffalo burgers, and then it's time to shoot some sporting clays. A local named Heath Roy—Stetson; craggy mountain features; an easy manner—takes us to the proving grounds and introduces us to our very first guns. Never having held a firearm before, I'm starting to feel like Elmer Fudd on a bad day. But we are set at ease by a family from Alabama, a middle-aged internist and his two sons, one a freshly minted Birmingham physics teacher, the other a red-haired little spark plug. The doctor proudly tells us that he gave his youngest his first gun when he turned five, to which I can only reply, "Oh." I pick up the weapon and Roy gives me some last-minute advice: "Pretend there's a pair of knees hangin' off that skeet. Shoot the knees." The recoil punches a pale yellow bruise into my chest, but I hit the target and the clay explodes like a minor firecracker. E. does "real good" too, while the young physics teacher barely misses a clay.

Soon, Roy is referring to me by the first syllable of my name—"Let me see your game face, Gar!"— and his patient advice on following through helps me hit a low-flying, ground-skimming rabbit. By

WHERE TO STAY

The Resort at Paws Up Rustic sophistication redefined, with 28 comfortable ranch homes and 12 luxe safari tents (only available when the seasonal River Camp accepts guests in warm weather). The resort is open for winter from mid-December through mid-February. *40060 Paws Up Rd., Greenough, Mont.; 800/473-0601 or 406/244-5200; pawsup.com; doubles from $$$$$, including meals.*

GETTING THERE

Though blissfully removed from civilization, the Resort at Paws Up is just 35 miles east of Missoula, Montana, where most carriers fly direct from hubs in Los Angeles, Seattle, Phoenix, Denver, Las Vegas, and Salt Lake City. Paws Up provides free shuttle transportation to and from the property.

Ranch staffers at the Resort at Paws Up's Saddle Club.

FIVE MORE WINTER LODGES

Cross-country skiing at Devil's Thumb Ranch, in Tabernash, Colorado.

TABERNASH, COLORADO
Lodge at Devil's Thumb Ranch At this updated, 5,000-acre compound, 65 miles from Denver, kids can play billiards and go candlepin bowling while parents unwind in the earth-toned Ranch Creek Spa, built from reclaimed pine and rockslide stones. Nordic ski trails cater to all levels—even the family dog can join—and movies play nightly in the 37-seat theater. *800/ 933-4339; devilsthumbranch. com; doubles from $$.*

DARBY, MONTANA
Triple Creek Ranch Adults-only resort on 600 acres in the Bitterroot Mountains. The 23 plush log cabins are outfitted with wood-burning fireplaces, hot tubs, and locally woven textiles. Itineraries are tailored to guests' interests and can include dinners at the chef's table, wine tastings, or helicopter tours. *800/654-2943 or 406/821-4600; triplecreekranch.com; doubles from $$$, all-inclusive.*

TETON VILLAGE, WYOMING
Snake River Lodge & Spa Most adventure lodges are geared for all seasons, but Snake River was built with winter in mind. Located at the base of Jackson Hole Mountain Resort, it encompasses more than 2,500 acres of skiing terrain on two mountains; guests have access to a private heated walkway that leads to the resort's new tram. Massages and water treatments are available at the five-story Avanyu spa. *866/975-7625 or 307/732-6000; snakeriverlodge.com; doubles from $.*

DIXVILLE NOTCH, NEW HAMPSHIRE
Balsams Grand Resort Hotel Set in the remote northern reaches of New Hampshire's Great North Woods, this bastion of Old Yankee gentility is one of the last of the fabled 19th-century New England resorts, where men still wear jackets to dinner. The 8,000-acre property is paradise for winter sports lovers, with its own ski mountain and 60 miles of cross-country trails,

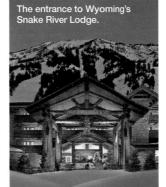

The entrance to Wyoming's Snake River Lodge.

as well as ice skating and snowshoeing. *800/255-0600; thebalsams.com; doubles from $, including meals.*

Horseback riding at Montana's Triple Creek Ranch.

LAKE PLACID, NEW YORK
Lake Placid Lodge Rebuilt after a fire in 2005 burned the original 1882 main house to the ground, the new five-suite, Arts and Crafts–style main lodge, which reopened in 2008, successfully evokes the property's Adirondack Great Camp roots. For utmost privacy, book one of the 19 lakeside log cabins built in the 1920's and 1930's, with their king-size feather beds, handcrafted furniture, and porches facing the water. (Ask for Whitney or Eagles Eyre.) Service is thoughtful and discreet, delivering bounteous breakfasts in wicker baskets and setting out fresh marsh-mallows and artisanal chocolate for s'mores by the fire pit at dusk. *877/523-2700 or 518/523-2700; lakeplacid lodge.com; doubles from $$$, including breakfast.*

KEY TO THE HOTEL PRICE ICONS $ UNDER $250 $$ $250–$499 $$$ $500–$749 $$$$ $750–$999 $$$$$ $1,000 AND UP

Photographed by Jessica Schwartzberg

HAWAII, REVISITED

FRESH FROM EXTENSIVE RENOVATIONS, TWO HISTORIC PROPERTIES—THE BIG ISLAND'S MAUNA KEA BEACH HOTEL AND THE ROYAL HAWAIIAN, ON WAIKIKI BEACH—ARE POISED TO RECAPTURE THEIR FORMER GLORY. BY MARIA SHOLLENBARGER

WHEN I WAS GROWING UP IN LOS ANGELES, MY PARENTS WOULD REGULARLY DECAMP

sans kids to the Mauna Kea. It was the first place they'd saved pennies to stay at as newlyweds, and it hosted them for anniversaries and much-needed escapes in the following decades. They'd come back sun-burnished, rejuvenated, and bearing the hotel's signature navy-and-white *yukata* for my brother and me to wear as bathrobes. By the time I was 13, I had ascribed to the place an enormous mystique: What was this magical hotel that returned my mom and dad to me looking, without fail, just a little bit like movie stars?

They weren't the only people in the 1970's on whom the magic rubbed off; the Mauna Kea was then the ne plus ultra of Hawaiian glamour and one of the top hotels in the world. Laurance Rockefeller, the founder of RockResorts, selected the site, overlooking the ivory crescent of Kaunaoa Beach on the then-pristine Kohala Coast; and he handpicked the architect—one Edward Charles Bassett of Skidmore, Owings, & Merrill—who erected in 1965 a series of dynamic horizontal spaces, stacked one atop the other, almost entirely unencumbered by walls to fully exploit views of the opalescent Pacific. To this buzz-generating building, Rockefeller bequeathed a museum-quality collection of Oceanic and Asian art, ranging from wooden Melanesian sculptures to life-size gilded Buddhas, which were scattered about in the open-air, tiled corridors.

Cut to 2005: the Mauna Kea had lost much of its cachet—aged to a comfortable, but not chic, family resort. Prince Resorts, which acquired the hotel in the eighties, wasn't oblivious to the hotel's faded interiors, and when an earthquake damaged the property in October 2006, management took advantage of the closure to stage a 15-month, $150 million renovation.

The results are subtle, and near pitch-perfect. The original 310 rooms and suites in the main building have been reduced to 258, layouts revised and enlarged. Understatement prevails—there are white-tile floors, white ceramic lamps and light fixtures, abstract and ethnic fabrics that reference Rockefeller's collections, and teak headboards. The rooms also have ingenious compartmentalized teak wall units that slide closed to conceal 42-inch flat-screen TV's (a concession to old-timers scandalized by the addition of *televisions* after all these years; the slick iPod alarm clocks and digital phones can't have pleased them much, either). Ocean-facing doubles acquired extra lanais, which are allocated to their bathrooms—white-on-white havens with deep soaking tubs and open rain showers. What could read as generic décor on first viewing soon reveals itself to be of exceptional quality—materials are all top-of-the-line and formidably expensive—and, in its aggregate aesthetic, to make subtle nods to both

OPPOSITE, CLOCKWISE FROM TOP LEFT: The Mauna Kea Beach Hotel's pool; inside the property's central atrium; *misoyaki* butterfish with *gobo*, bok choy, and *beurre fondu* at the hotel's Manta restaurant; a guest room. PREVIOUS SPREAD, FROM LEFT: A hibiscus at the Royal Hawaiian; the hotel's iconic façade.

the building's Midcentury heritage and the hotel's Asian-influenced ethos.

A small but lovely spa, managed by Bali-based Mandara, has been built in the former members' club room. The restaurant, Manta, has a new display kitchen and a refined, locally influenced menu that's heavy on excellent raw-bar offerings (with attendant prices); but its outdoor tables are

THE SHAG HAS DISAPPEARED; THE HIBISCUS-PINK PAINT JOB SAYS *ALOHA*, BUT THE VERNACULAR IS PURE RODEO DRIVE

positioned, as ever, for prime viewing of the mantas that feed at night below the terrace. And the beachside Hau Tree bar still serves the Ovaltine Froth milk shake—the singular deliciousness of which merits 45 years on a menu.

"IT'S LITTLE," SAYS THE GIRL PLAYING IN THE sand next to me, studying the rosy dimensions of the six-story Royal Hawaiian. Well, not really—it has 529 rooms, two restaurants, a spa, and a lobby shopping arcade that could accommodate a soccer match—but I see what she means: viewed from the beach, the Pink Palace, as it's also called, is so dwarfed by the towering forest of glass and steel bristling up around it as to evoke a generalized nostalgia for some Gilded Era of Waikiki Beach Past.

The Royal Hawaiian was constructed in 1927, 32 years before Hawaii achieved statehood, and has a guest roster that reads like a roll call of America's rich, famous, and Pennsylvania Avenue–dwelling. It's the home of the mai tai (first perfected at the hotel bar of the same name) and sits on the prime stretch of America's most famous beach: wide, quiet, perfect for outrigger and longboard approaches.

But Honolulu has grown up, and as the Kahala and the Halekulani and even the sleek new Trump International Hotel Beach Walk arrived, it became increasingly clear that the green shag in the guest rooms wasn't cutting it. So Starwood hotels (whose Luxury Collection division reflagged the Royal

Hawaiian in January 2009) set itself the task of recasting all that venerable history in a vibrant 21st-century light.

The shag has disappeared; the sleeked-up Mai Tai Bar now serves a killer ahi sashimi salad. The building's Spanish-Moorish good looks (that hibiscus-pink paint job says *aloha*, but the vernacular is pure Rodeo Drive) have been exploited to their best effect. The wide lanai facing the storied Coconut Grove, sectioned off from the main lobby decades ago, has been refurbished and reopened to the building. Now, guests are welcomed with an unbroken view from the hotel's porte cochère entrance past massive pink columns all the way to those sun-dappled palms, which you can see from the polished koa check-in desks. Around the corner from the grove, billowing white cabanas set among gardens house the new Abhasa Spa's alfresco massage suites.

The rooms strike a balance between traditional island-ethnic and modern without sliding into either kitsch or blandness. The regular appearance of a metallic pineapple print on a poppy-pink background (on the walls and as upholstery), admittedly a bit dubious-sounding on paper, is actually a rather charming, David Hicks–ian conceit. Some of the junior suites are hampered by small bathrooms, a holdover from original construction—how did Henry Ford/Douglas Fairbanks/the Shah of Iran countenance such cramped quarters?—though the designers have done an admirable job of dressing them up with marble and state-of-the-art fixtures.

Then there's the knockout restaurant, Azure, which merits a visit regardless of where in town you stay—preferably after dark, when the enormous suspended Moroccan lanterns are lit, their light flickering off the coffered white ceilings. The room is well and truly chic (not just chic "for Hawaii"), and chef Jon Matsubara has a masterful hand with the seafood, which comes straight from the fish auction building at Pier 38. If your tastes hew more toward pig, order the sublime baby back ribs in a Kona coffee marinade. They're the familiar, made sophisticated and satisfying with a studied twist of good taste. The new Hawaii, really.

OPPOSITE, CLOCKWISE FROM TOP LEFT: Ahi *poke* with taro chips and the signature drink at the Royal Hawaiian's Mai Tai Bar; the hotel's lobby; a surf instructor in front of the Royal Beach Club; a view of Waikiki Beach from the hotel.

KAUAI

OAHU
Honolulu
Waikiki Beach

MAUI

Kawaihae
Harbor

Hawi
Paauilo
Kohala
Coast
Waimea
Hilo
Kailua-Kona

HAWAII

Mauna Kea Beach Hotel, on the Big Island.

WHERE TO STAY
BIG ISLAND
Mauna Kea Beach Hotel
Understated and refined, with a legendary golf course and a new spa. *62-100 Mauna Kea Beach Dr., Kohala Coast; 866/977-4589 or 808/882-7222; maunakeabeachhotel.com; doubles from $$.*

OAHU
Royal Hawaiian, a Luxury Collection Resort Built in 1927 on the most storied beach in the U.S.; the renovation successfully balances island nostalgia and contemporary chic. *2259 Kalakaua Ave., Honolulu; 800/325-3589 or 808/923-7311; royal-hawaiian. com; doubles from $$$.*

WHERE TO EAT + DRINK
BIG ISLAND
Bamboo Restaurant & Gallery
Supremely laid-back, with tasty fare like plump pot stickers and baby back ribs barbecued in spicy passion fruit. *Akoni Pule Hwy., Hawi; 808/889-5555; dinner for two XXX.*

Blue Dragon Coastal Cuisine & Musiquarium Open-air nightclub with live music. *61-3616 Kawaihae Rd., Kawaihae Harbor; 808/882-7771; dinner for two XXX.*

Brown's Beach House Fresh seafood and traditional Hawaiian cuisine in an elegant setting just steps from the shore. *Fairmont Orchid, 1 N. Kaniku Dr., Kohala Coast; 808/885-2000; dinner for two XXX.*

Huggo's Family-owned seafood institution with a lively open-air bar overlooking the ocean. *75-5828 Kahakai Rd., Kailua-Kona; 808/329-1493; dinner for two XXX.*

Merriman's Restaurant
Hawaiian regional cuisine from nationally lauded chef Peter Merriman, who pairs locally sourced dishes with high-quality wines. *65-1227 Opelo Rd., Waimea; 808/885-6822; dinner for two XXX.*

Pahu ia Extravagant outdoor dining with expansive waterfront views. *Four Seasons Resort Hualalai, 72-100 Kaupulehu Dr., Kailua-Kona; 808/325-8000; dinner for two XXXX.*

OAHU
Diamond Head Market & Grill
Takeout favorite renowned for its tangy Korean barbecued chicken. *3158 Monsarrat Ave., Honolulu; 808/732-0077; lunch for two XX.*

House Without a Key Grab a potent mai tai at this historic beachfront bar and restaurant. *Halekulani, 2199 Kalia Rd., Honolulu; 808/923-2311; dinner for two XX.*

Indigo Eurasian-influenced dishes—including spicy jumbo shrimp with saffron rice and pineapple chutney—make up the menu at this trendy yet tasteful Chinatown establishment. *1121 Nuuanu Ave., Honolulu; 808/521-2900; dinner for two XXX.*

Irifune Quirky, hole-in-the-wall Japanese joint known for serving some of the best ahi tuna in town. *563 Kapahulu Ave., Honolulu; 808/737-1141; dinner for two XX.*

La Mariana Sailing Club
One of the last old-school tiki bars, where the tropical drinks are generous and the kitschy atmosphere is straight out of

Pahu ia, on the Big Island.

House Without a Key, in Honolulu.

1950's Hawaii. *50 Sand Island Access Rd., Honolulu; 808/848-2800; drinks for two* ✘.

Rainbow Drive-In Lunchtime staple since 1961; surfboard-topped vans, chili dogs, and slush floats are de rigueur. *3308 Kanaina Ave., Honolulu; 808/737-0177; lunch for two* ✘.

WHAT TO SEE + DO
BIG ISLAND
Big Island Eco Adventures Take a 40-minute off-road safari followed by an eight-zipline descent through the tree canopy.

808/889-5111; bigislandeco adventures.com.

Hawaii Forest & Trail Book a private helicopter tour and waterfall walk with this award-winning eco-outfitter. *808/331-8505; hawaii-forest.com.*

Hawaiian Vanilla Co. Elegantly restored structure and vanilla plant on the slopes of Mauna Kea, against a backdrop of lush farmland and tropical rain forest; hosts tastings, luncheons, and traditional up-country teas with tours of the farm and factory. *43-2007 Paauilo Mauka Rd., Paauilo; 808/776-1771; hawaiianvanilla.com.*

Kona Honu Divers Snorkel or dive among the breathtaking nocturnal manta rays as their underwater ballet is illuminated with floodlights. *808/324-4668; konahonudivers.com.*

OAHU
Bishop Museum Victorian-style building that houses one of the world's most renowned collections of Polynesian art and artifacts, along with an impressive array of natural-history specimens. *1525 Bernice St., Honolulu; 808/847-3511; bishopmuseum.org.*

Shangri La Opulent former residence of tobacco heiress Doris Duke; now a museum with more than 3,500 rare works of Islamic art, including furniture, wood, enamel, ceramics, and decorative doors. *4055 Papu Circle, Honolulu; 808/532-3853; shangrilahawaii.org.*

Waikiki Beach Walk Eight acres that have been transformed from a seedy strip into a modern-day promenade, thanks to $585 million in private funds. *Honolulu; waikikibeachwalk.com.*

Shangri La, in Honolulu.

FOUR MORE NEWLY REFRESHED GRANDE DAMES

CALIFORNIA
L'Auberge Del Mar
A favored haunt for Hollywood heavy-hitters like Charlie Chaplin; abandoned in 1969 and rebuilt 20 years later as a nod to the original's glory days. The property recently received a $26 million face-lift that added a spa and restaurant and created an open-air lobby. *1540 Camino Del Mar, Del Mar; 800/245-9757 or 858/259-1515; laubergedel mar.com; doubles from $$.*

FLORIDA
Ritz-Carlton, Palm Beach
Classic old-guard getaway with an expanded oceanfront terrace, two restaurants, and 42 suites that each underwent $100,000 revamps—not to mention Eau Spa, a 42,000-square-foot playground of gardens and treatment rooms. *100 S. Ocean Blvd., Manalapan; 800/241-3333 or 561/533-6000; ritzcarlton.com; doubles from $$.*

HAWAII
St. Regis Princeville Resort
After a multimillion dollar renovation, this former Sheraton emerged as St. Regis's first Hawaiian property in 2009 with a 11,000-square-foot spa, a Jean-Georges Vongerichten restaurant, and the hotel brand's signature butler service. *5520 Ka Haku Rd., Princeville, Kauai; 877/787-3447 or 808/826-9644; stregisprinceville.com; doubles from $$$.*

NEW YORK
c/o the Maidstone
Historic, *Gatsby*esque retreat taken over by Swedish hotelier Jenny Ljungberg's boutique brand, c/o Hotels, in spring 2009. Eclectic Scandinavian interiors and eco-friendly Malin & Goetz toiletries join private wine cellars and a Slow Food–inspired restaurant. *207 Main St., East Hampton; 631/324-5006; themaidstone.com; doubles from $$.*

KEY TO THE DINING PRICE ICONS   ✘ UNDER $25   ✘✘ $25–$74   ✘✘✘ $75–$149   ✘✘✘✘ $150–$299   ✘✘✘✘✘ $300 AND UP

Chopped pork shoulder at Lexington Barbecue, in Lexington, North Carolina.

Cheeses from Cowgirl Creamery & Cantina, in Marin County, California.

A grape picker at Seven Hills Winery, in Walla Walla, Washington.

Spinach soup at Francine Bistro, in Camden, Maine.

OOD + DRINK

MAINE COURSE

BEYOND THE CRAB SHACKS AND THE LOBSTER-ROLL JOINTS, THERE'S EVEN MORE GREAT FOOD TO BE FOUND IN MAINE—RESTAURANTS WITH SPATCHCOCKED HARLEQUIN QUAIL, DUCK-CONFIT PANINO, AND KOLA-NUT FROTH ON THE MENU. (AND YES, THE LOBSTER ROLLS ARE SUPERB.) BY PETER JON LINDBERG

WE BOUGHT 14 OF THE HEIRLOOM TOMATOES, WITH THOUGHTS OF A SEASIDE PICNIC.'

We meant to stop at eight—two each—but couldn't help ourselves. They were the most glorious tomatoes, showing every hue from bottle green to burgundy, and heavy with juice, like water balloons on the verge of bursting. The idea was to save them till Kennebunkport, three hours away.

That notion lasted 20 minutes. We had no plates, but we had a plastic knife. In the backseat, our friend Laura sliced the tomatoes in half and handed them out for us to tip back, squeeze, and drink, then devour whole. The tomatoes were from Chase's Daily, a farm stand-slash-restaurant-slash-revelation in Belfast, Maine. I would call them the best midday snack of our trip—but then, we'd said the same about yesterday's crab roll, and the previous day's Camembert, and the previous afternoon's oysters.

I was in the midst of a two-week culinary tour of the Maine coast. As fortification I had brought along my wife, Nilou, and two food-obsessed friends. Mark is from New England, but Laura, a California native, had never been north of Boston. Our goal was to convert her to the cult of Maine. Me, I grew up 20 minutes from the beaches of York and Ogunquit. What taco stands were to Laura's youth, lobster pounds were to mine.

Lobster is still the go-to order here, but there's so much more to Maine's pantry: artisanal breads and farmstead cheeses, zesty herbs and buttery greens, gold-glowing squash blossoms and sweet corn, wild mushrooms and blueberries. Even the humblest kitchens have access to luscious peekytoe crab, plump mussels, and absurdly fresh fish.

What Maine also has, more than ever before, is a roster of talented chefs who are redefining local cooking. Sure, plenty of restaurants still dish out retro Yankee resort food (maple-glazed salmon, potato-crusted lamb) for people like, say, George and Barbara Bush, whose portraits hang by the door. Now, however, you can find a bold and inventive contemporary cuisine that never places novelty before flavor, gimmickry over essence.

But hold up. First I have to tell you about the oysters.

DROWNING, WITH SHALLOTS

The Damariscotta River is a tidal estuary that juts into Maine's central coast. Two thousand years ago, oysters thrived here; along the banks remain vast shell middens left by Native American tribes. By the 1970's the oysters were long gone. Yet to a handful of aqua-farmers, the Damariscotta seemed an ideal spot for cultivation: today the river yields 2–3 million oysters each year.

One of those pioneers was Dick Clime, who founded Dodge Cove Marine Farm in 1977. To my mind, those oysters are the finest in New England. Strong and hardy, the bivalves also retain their water (or "liquor") exceptionally well. The harvest finds its way to restaurants across the nation, but I've never had fresher ones than at Scales, a winning little raw bar in Portland. Knocking back a Dodge Cove was like diving headfirst into the ocean and being walloped by a wave—a bracing, briny shot of the chilly Atlantic, backed by a captivating sweetness and the tingle of the house mignonette. "It's like drowning, with shallots," was Mark's euphoric description. Sadly, the restaurant has since closed; its owner, Sam Hayward (more on him later), is currently seeking a new location.

Portland, the state's biggest city, claims to have

OPPOSITE: A Kennebunk fisherman with his day's catch. PREVIOUS SPREAD, FROM LEFT: Steamed lobster at MC Perkins Cove, in Ogunquit; a dockside lobster shack on Cape Porpoise, near Kennebunkport.

IN GOD WE TRUST
NATIVE ★ TOMATOES : CORN \
CUKES: BEETS / GREEN BEANS
BREAD-PIES-JAM \ MUMS: APPLES

as many restaurants per capita as San Francisco, which may or may not be true. For a city of only 64,000, it certainly has more than its share of great ones. Ever since the 1980's, when quirky bistros such as Café Always and Alberta's were raising the bar on New England cooking, Portland has been a magnet for aspiring chefs. What's not to love, after all? With its mix of stately roseate façades and dingy sailors' haunts, its brine-reeking wharves and its I. M. Pei & Partners–designed art museum, Portland nicely straddles the line between highbrow and hardscrabble.

The city's most inspired cooking can be found at Hugo's, where chef Rob Evans's technique owes much to the bold inventions of Thomas Keller. (Evans worked at Keller's French Laundry in Napa before moving to Portland and taking over Hugo's in 2000.) Forgive the 80's-kitsch interior and focus your attention on the food, which is arty, strange, and utterly luxurious. First up for us: an espresso cup rimmed with popcorn dust (!), containing a shot of lobster-and-corn bisque laced with chorizo oil. Next came Evans's masterstroke: an heirloom-tomato plate, in theory, except the tomatoes were delicately peeled, accompanied by a quivering, silken *panna cotta* of lemon olive oil and tomato water, then dressed with white anchovies and a Thai-basil–infused vinaigrette.

Evans riffs on familiar combinations—say, lamb in mint sauce, with carrots and squash—only in novel forms. In this case, the lamb saddle came with a luscious carrot mousse and a spearmint-zucchini "cake." Both side dishes were like understudies outshining the original cast. Therein lies Evans's talent: his creations seem hypercerebral on paper (it took our waitress 37 seconds to "explain" the duck) but are ultimately about pure flavor. Meanwhile, ingredients that sound extraneous are revealed as essential. Take that duck, for instance—the breast cooked *sous vide*, the leg slow-roasted, both tender and moist—paired with golden beets and spiced plums. The fundamentals were excellent. Add the surprising crunch of diced water chestnuts and the complementary bitterness of kola-nut froth, and the dish was transcendent.

I visit Portland several times a year and go to Fore Street whenever I'm in town—not to trace the culinary vanguard but to be sated with honest, earthbound cooking. Over a 14-year run, Fore Street has become Maine's answer to Chez Panisse, with chef Sam Hayward (who also ran Scales) as Alice Waters—champion of local producers,

WHAT MAINE HAS, MORE THAN EVER BEFORE, IS A ROSTER OF TALENTED CHEFS WHO ARE REDEFINING LOCAL COOKING

proponent of sustainable fishing and farming, sultan of the greenmarket. For Maine farmers, a name check on Fore Street's menu is equivalent to a spot in an Oscar-party gift bag.

Even on weeknights, you might wait an hour for one of Fore Street's copper-topped walk-in tables. Faded brick walls, burlap sacks, and unfinished beams set the tone in the dining room, a former garage for oil tankers. The male clientele is clad in regulation New England guy-wear—Top-Siders; Red Sox caps; khaki shorts with belts. (Ahh, my people!) In the open kitchen a half-dozen cooks, also wearing Sox caps, tend to flame-licked turnspits and stoke a roaring brick oven.

Out of that 900-degree oven come Fore Street's famous roasted mussels, shrouded in steam: juicy, raft-cultured gems from nearby Bangs Island. "We're so spoiled by Maine mussels that we never use anyone else's," Hayward says. "If they're not available, we just take mussels off the menu." Splashed with vermouth and cooked with garlic-and-lemon butter, parsley, and toasted almonds, they're the platonic ideal of shellfish.

Despite Fore Street's proximity to the sea—the misty wharves are visible through the windows—Hayward's menu focuses on meat and fowl. We were wowed by spatchcocked, wood-grilled harlequin quail. *Spatchcocked* means the bird is butterflied to allow for faster cooking time and moister meat. Dryness was a nonissue, however, since the quail had also been basted in a stock of shiitakes, veal, and duck fat, then finished with I-don't-want-to-know-how-much butter. Bring Lipitor; the result is fabulous and worth the risk.

In Portland's highly democratic dining scene, Erik Desjarlais's cooking can be described as

OPPOSITE: Breakfast at Chase's Daily, in Belfast. PREVIOUS SPREAD, CLOCKWISE FROM TOP LEFT: A plate of just-finished local oysters; an Arnold Palmer served in a Mason jar at Duckfat, in Portland; tea-brined duck at Francine Bistro, in Camden; Kennebunkport's rugged coastline; owners Matt James and Alison Pray at Portland's Standard Baking Co.; Browne Trading Market, in Portland; a roadside sign touting what's fresh; lobsterman Bobby Daggett in Cape Porpoise.

defiantly uncasual. Desjarlais opened Bandol in 2003, when he was just 26. Despite rave reviews, his often brilliant $69 tasting menus—with their predilection for offal—never found a wide audience

OVER A 14-YEAR RUN, FORE STREET HAS BECOME MAINE'S ANSWER TO CHEZ PANISSE, WITH CHEF SAM HAYWARD AS ALICE WATERS

in Portland. Nor did the hushed, Vivaldian tone of the dining room. (Desjarlais has since abandoned the original space, reopening Bandol as Evangeline, a French brasserie with a local twist.)

At the original Bandol we were knocked out by three—count 'em, three—amuses-bouches, including a sublime fried oyster in a cucumber consommé. The pan-roasted sweetbreads were remarkably light; the succulent leg of lamb was matched with a delightful cassoulet of leeks and cranberry beans. But the highlight was Desjarlais's way with the cheese course. Translucent plum slices, like shards of stained glass, complemented a wedge of creamy, mushroomy Constant Bliss from Vermont. A sharp Neal's Yard Cheshire came drizzled with wildflower honey and scattered with diced pear. Even the fig tart was topped with a dollop of chalky-yet-sweet chèvre ice cream.

A recent trend in Portland involves big-name chefs who are starting casual lunch spots. Rob Evans of Hugo's finds his outlet at Duckfat, an eatery that's as homey as Hugo's is refined: bar stools, rose stems in Coke bottles, and a communal Magnetic Poetry board (current entry: I AM NOT YOUR TROUSERS). The kitchen is staffed by friendly dudes in cargo shorts who crank My Morning Jacket while assembling the city's best sandwiches, including a fall-apart duck-confit panino with black-currant chutney. There are also fries, twice cooked in duck fat and seasoned with a powder of dried capers, onions, parsley, and garlic—umami heaven in a paper cone. And for dessert, a root-beer float made with Duckfat's fizzy concoction of Italian soda water and sassafras. Add two scoops of fragrant vanilla ice cream from Smiling Hill Farm, and presto—a tumblerful of childhood.

Smiling Hill Farm, it turned out, was just a 10-minute drive from downtown Portland. It's been owned by the Knight family since the 1700's, but only recently has its dairy been gaining broader renown. Besides that fantastic ice cream, Danny Meyer sources Smiling Hill's butter for his restaurant the Modern, in New York. The farm is also home to one of Maine's top cheese makers, Silvery Moon Creamery.

A HEAD OF CABBAGE

Farther up the coast, Maine's shoreline becomes craggier and the Atlantic breezes more insistent, and one's thoughts inevitably turn to...sauerkraut. Generations have made the pilgrimage to Morse's Sauerkraut, a little red farmhouse in North Waldoboro.

This area was settled by German immigrants adept at farming and fermenting cabbage. Continuing in this tradition was Virgil Morse, who began selling his sauerkraut commercially in 1918; his family kept up the business for decades until David Swetnam and Jacquelyn Sawyer took over in 2000. Not much has changed.

The best sauerkraut is made from sweet, ivory-hued "winter" cabbage, which holds its flavor better than its more attractive, green-tinged cousin. Here it's fermented in plastic drums in a frigid storage room, slowing down the process—"the longer it takes to make, the better the kraut," says Swetnam—then transferred to wooden barrels. The genial staff will scoop out pints into flimsy plastic tubs that inevitably leak when you carry them on to, say, an airplane. (Trust me on this.) No matter: the result is tangy and assertive, clean and still crunchy. This is raw, unpasteurized, "live" kraut, almost too good to use as a mere garnish.

BACK TO THE GARDEN

A salad is a salad, you say. But not in Maine, not in late summer. The salad that the four of us had at Primo was, by any measure, above and beyond. On the surface it was an unassuming tangle of summer lettuces, subtly dressed with a red-wine vinaigrette. But tucked within the greens were powerful herbs from Primo's own garden—verbena, basil, mint, fennel, cinnamon basil—so that each forkful was like slamming hits of herbal

extract. Mark sat dumbfounded for minutes, ruminating over a *shiso* leaf.

If chef and co-owner Melissa Kelly weren't a star in her own right, her garden could carry the day. I've followed Kelly since she was at the Old Chatham Sheepherding Inn, near the Berkshires. After leaving in 1999, she and her then-fiancé, pastry chef Price Kushner, ended up in Rockland, Maine, where they bought and renovated a gingerbread Victorian, carving out several homey dining rooms across two floors. Primo (named for Kelly's grandfather from Bologna) is nominally an Italian restaurant, though not so you'd recognize it. Consider Kelly's take on, er, spaghetti and meatballs: bright-green arugula linguine cooked al dente and an ethereal tomato-veal-and-pork *ragù* topped with feathery wisps of fennel. Every dish manages to seem light and delicate while carrying the most robust and assertive flavors—none more so than what comes from that magnificent garden.

Kelly gets the bulk of attention from out-of-staters, but another young chef has been causing a stir in nearby Camden. One of the nation's most photogenic seaside resorts, Camden remains a favored retreat for the Rockefellers and their ilk. Most chefs up here remain stuck in Ye Olde New England mode—but not Brian Hill of Francine Bistro. Hill got his start in Boston, working under Todd English at Olives; after stints in Los Angeles, Hawaii, and New York, he washed up in Camden in 2002 and took a job at Francine. Back then it was just a modest 25-seat café with a single hot plate for a stove. This didn't stop Hill from dazzling local foodies with improbable hot-plate feasts. Hill eventually bought the place, installed a proper kitchen, and drew a devoted following. The night we stopped in, there was an hour wait for a table; James Rockefeller Jr. was ahead of us in line. But Francine is hardly posh. The wooden tables were bare except for tiny planters of chive blossoms.

Hill sources most of his ingredients at the Camden farmers' market, including broiler chickens from Maine-ly Poultry, in Warren; organic beef from Caldwell Farms, in Turner ("the finest I've tasted, anywhere," Hill raves); and wild-foraged chanterelles from the Oyster Creek

A fillet of flounder at Fore Street, in Portland, above left. RIGHT: The restaurant's open kitchen.

Mushroom Company, in Damariscotta. Like me, Hill is obsessed with fungi. "Maine's chanterelles are actually better than the European variety—they give off this intense apricot-jam aroma the second they hit the pan," he says. "Black trumpets, too.

SHAFTS OF SUNLIGHT STREAM THROUGH THE TALL WINDOWS, ILLUMINATING BINS OF VEGETABLES LIKE SOME RAY-OF-GOD TABLEAU

I've never found anything as satisfying as truffles, but these come closest to that big, animal flavor." That evening the black trumpets found their way into a marvelously savory spinach soup. A cluster of oyster mushrooms lent a peppery bite to the sautéed calamari. Hill's cooking is rooted less in the sea than in the funky flavors of the earth; for instance, the powerful tastes of rosemary and braised bacon that accompanied the seared scallops.

Odd coincidence: before he donned his chef's whites, Hill was the guitarist for Heretix, one of Boston's great unsung bands and a favorite of mine and Mark's back in college. We both recognized him as soon as he stepped out of the kitchen: "Wait, weren't you...?" Hill was a talented guitarist, but he's even better behind the stoves—alt-rock's loss, gastronomy's gain.

THE OTHER HARD SHELL

The cove-studded, wildflower-laced Blue Hill Peninsula is famous as the home turf of E. B. White, Helen and Scott Nearing, and Robert McCloskey, who together go a long way in describing the region's bucolic appeal as well as its demographic. Pottery studios, antiques emporiums, glassblowers' studios, yarn boutiques: Blue Hill is heaven for some, twee for others, and absolute hell for anyone between the ages of 6 and 22. I was a sixth grader when my parents first dragged me here on vacation, and besides the cool sailboats, the only thing that kept me from bolting was the crab rolls.

Smaller than the familiar Jonah crabs, peekytoe crabs are endemic to Maine and proliferate in the inshore waters around Blue Hill. Until recently, sand crabs were reviled as worthless pests with a penchant for stealing lobster bait; fishermen called them "picked toes" for the shape of the two hind legs, and usually tossed them back. Then, in the early 1980's, Rod Mitchell, founder, along with his wife, Cynde, of Portland's Browne Trading Market, discovered how tasty picked-toe crabmeat could be when cooked and shelled correctly. "Of course, the name wasn't very appealing, so I started selling them as 'peeky-toe,'" he recalls. A quarter-century later, peekytoe has become a prized catch; Mainers will tell you it's even sweeter than lobster. "Wish I'd patented the name," Mitchell says with a laugh.

Around Blue Hill, everyone's got a favorite crab joint—Crosby's, in Bucksport, or Jordan's, over in Ellsworth—but you can find a great peekytoe roll anywhere. Take the Bayview Market & Takeout, a screen-doored trailer on Route 175 in Penobscot, where owner Larry Reynolds greets you in a Down East drawl so extreme you wonder if he's putting you on.

To mix the perfect martini, Winston Churchill would reputedly glance across the room at a bottle of vermouth and then pour the gin. The same idea holds for a crab roll. Unadorned peekytoe meat is sweet and creamy enough; any mayo should remain sealed in the jar. Reynolds will add Miracle Whip, but go ahead and tell him there's no need. Mixed only with a little pepper and served on a toasted hot-dog bun, his crab roll is outstanding—and a bona fide bargain.

THE FARMERS AND THEIR DAUGHTERS

The harbor town of Belfast is one of Maine's overlooked showpieces. Its sloping main street is lined with neo-Gothic and Neoclassical architecture; candy-cane barber poles and soda fountains still occupy the ornate storefronts. But don't take its primness as mere tourist fodder: Belfast is a vital working town, and Chase's Daily is its buzzing hub.

The Chase family—father Addison, mother Penny, and daughters Megan and Phoebe—owns a 500-acre farm in nearby Freedom. That's right, Freedom. Six years ago they took over Belfast's 1888 Odd Fellows Hall, whose ground level is a plank-floored, tin-ceilinged warehouse space. It now resembles a downtown gallery; funky artwork hangs on the brick walls. A 49-seat restaurant

occupies the front half. Out back is a retail market selling produce from the Chases' farm. Shafts of sunlight stream through the tall windows, illuminating bins of vegetables like some ray-of-God tableau: scarlet and fuchsia turnip greens, yellow and purple baby carrots. I challenge you to locate a more tantalizing assortment of produce, outside of a Dutch still life. (This was where we found the aforementioned killer tomatoes.)

The all-day restaurant and bakery fills up with an eclectic crowd: farmers; Feldenkrais practitioners; meter maids on coffee breaks. Three of the waitresses when we visited were ruddy-cheeked farm girls; the other had a Bettie Page tattoo. We came for breakfast (omelettes with roasted sweet onions, sautéed Swiss chard, and fontina) and, not believing our luck, returned two hours later for lunch (a frothy, chilled soup of potato, leek, and fennel, sprinkled with zesty chives—all of it from the Chases' farm). Only after we left did we realize that everything on the menu was vegetarian.

LOCATION, LOCATION, LOCATION

Maine is blessed with a thousand knockout restaurant locations but never enough restaurateurs to properly exploit them. The exception: MC Perkins Cove, in the tidy resort of Ogunquit, site of Maine's finest sand beach. Perkins Cove itself is an uncannily pretty harbor, with a whitewashed wooden drawbridge that's cranked up by hand when a tall mast glides in.

For years, this location—the best spot in the Cove—was occupied by the late and not-at-all-lamented Hurricanes, which stood on a rocky promontory with views across tidal pools to the ocean. In the spring of 2003 the site was taken over by chefs Mark Gaier and Clark Frasier (hence the initials in the restaurant's new name), who earned national renown at Arrows, also in Ogunquit. Over the course of two decades I've had great meals at Arrows, but on a more recent visit I found the food overthought, overpriced, and underwhelming. MC Perkins Cove goes for the more casual vibe of a seafood shack and succeeds admirably.

Boats at Portland harbor, above.

The two-story space is nearly all windows, with minimal decoration (that view is drama enough). Service is assured and unforced. And the kitchen works magic with coastal classics: luscious crab cakes; steamed mussels; plank-roasted cod. Gaier

IT'S BEEN SAID BY EVERY FOOD WRITER WHO EVER PASSED THROUGH HERE, BUT THE CLAM SHACK'S LOBSTER ROLL REALLY IS THE BEST

and Frasier have a knack for sourcing superb ingredients (the double-tiered shellfish tower is remarkably fresh), while most of the produce comes from the vast garden at Arrows. The chefs inject just enough creativity to keep things interesting. Take the deconstructed clam chowder: a timbale of succulent clams and herbed potatoes forms an island in the buttery milk broth, which is topped with a swirl of paprika oil and a sprig of fragrant thyme. I grew up on the chowder served at Barnacle Billy's down the street—but the reinvention at MC Perkins Cove made me consider switching sides.

LOBSTER, UPSCALE

Look, I love lobster as much as—no, way more than—the next guy. I come from a line of New Englanders who eat the slimy green tomalley and knock back "claw shots" to savor the remaining juice. But I'll admit that lobster doesn't dress up well. Maine menus are rife with whimsical takes—lobster spring rolls, lobster nachos, etc.—but do any chefs improve on the classic, saltwater-steamed preparation? Hardly ever.

Jonathan Cartwright does. The chef at Kennebunk's White Barn Inn restaurant has developed a repertoire of inventive lobster riffs that are clever but never cloying. Funny, too, because WBI is a resolutely old-school place, with linen-topped tables and a tuxedoed pianist. The menu spells out the prices ("ninety-five dollars" for a four-course prix fixe). Jackets are required; if you forget yours, they'll issue you a spare—invariably navy with brass buttons. And service is impeccably formal: our waiter said things like, "I'll give you a moment to explore the menu," then returned to ask, "Are you tempted to

OPPOSITE: A bowl of clam chowder from the Clam Shack, in Kennebunkport.

enjoy anything you see?" It's a throwback in every way, except for Cartwright's cooking.

You can order lobster for every course and never tire of the flavor. Our meal began with a sensational amuse-bouche: a coddled egg served in the shell with poached lobster medallions and a subtle, not-too-sweet maple compote. Next was a zesty lobster gazpacho, sharpened with roasted pine nuts and accompanied by a miniature lobster roll on warm brioche. A powerful grapefruit sorbet served as a palate cleanser (another retro touch). Then came Cartwright's signature dish: a 1¾-pound lobster removed from its shell and steamed in a reduction of Cognac, cream, butter, and coral (lobster roe), then served atop a nest of white fettuccine with snow peas, carrots, and ginger. The dish is richer than the couple at the next table and ridiculously good.

LOBSTER, DOWN-HOME

But let's face it: coddled eggs and Cognac are kind of cheating, no? Sometimes you simply need a great lobster roll. For that, you head a quarter-mile down the road and queue up at the Clam Shack, next to the Kennebunkport Bridge. It's been said by every food writer who ever passed through here, but the Clam Shack's lobster roll really is the best in Maine. Actually, it's tied for first with the one from Red's Eats, another roadside stand up the coast, in Wiscasset. Both are generously filled (Red's uses the meat of a one-pound lobster per sandwich). And each comes with your choice of mayo or drawn butter—or, if you're insane, both. The two spots make a point of shredding the meat by hand instead of by knife, to avoid the taint of oxidation; the resulting morsels are pleasingly intact and clean-tasting.

The benches outside were occupied, so we ate the rolls while leaning against the railing of the bridge, watching the yachts and sailboats bob gently in the Kennebunkport Marina, alternating hits of salty air with tangy, sweet bites of lobster. In the end, it was the Clam Shack lobster roll that proved the tipping point in our Maine-indoctrination experiment: Laura was thoroughly converted. Then and there, the four of us decided to head back for another go-round the following month. See you at Chase's—and, for God's sake, save us some tomatoes.

DOWN EAST FEAST: 19 classic Maine tastes

1 Crab roll, **Bayview Market & Takeout** (Penobscot)

2 Heirloom tomato salad, **Chase's Daily** (Belfast)

3 Blueberries, **Sewalls Orchard** (Lincolnville)

4 Foraged mushrooms, **Francine Bistro** (Camden)

5 House-grown greens, **Primo** (Rockland)

6 Sauerkraut, **Morse's Sauerkraut** (North Waldoboro)

7 Lobster roll, **Red's Eats** (Wiscasset)

8 Camembert, **Silvery Moon Creamery** (Westbrook)

9 Gingerbread, **Standard Baking Co.** (Portland)

10 Lamb-and-feta flatbread, **Five Fifty-Five** (Portland)

11 Olive-oil *panna cotta*, **Hugo's** (Portland)

12 Belgian *frites*, **Duckfat** (Portland)

13 Mussels, **Fore Street** (Portland)

14 Smoked salmon, **Browne Trading Market** (Portland)

15 Lobster, **White Barn Inn** (Kennebunk)

16 Fried clams, the **Clam Shack** (Kennebunkport)

17 Vegetable soup, **Joshua's** (Wells)

18 Classic clam chowder, **Barnacle Billy's** (Ogunquit)

19 Deconstructed clam chowder, **MC Perkins Cove** (Ogunquit)

Hidden Pond, in Kennebunkport.

GETTING THERE + AROUND

All of the places mentioned in this story are within a three-hour drive north or south of Portland (Maine's largest city). Portland International Jetport is served by Continental Airlines, Delta Air Lines, JetBlue, United Airlines, and US Airways. There's also a decent airport in Bangor that's more convenient to Camden, Rockport, and Blue Hill.

WHERE TO STAY

Hidden Pond Upscale yet slightly whimsical camp on 60 wooded acres, with 14 two-bedroom cottages that provide the perfect breezy summer escape. *354 Goose Rocks Rd., Kennebunkport;* 888/967-9050 or 207/967-9050; *hiddenpondmaine.com; cottages from $$$.*

Inn at Sunrise Point The most stylish and best situated of the Camden area's inns—a porch-rimmed 1920's mansion that overlooks a broad, sloping lawn and glittering Penobscot Bay. The best rooms are in the five outlying cottages, each with a fireplace and spacious deck (the Winslow Homer cottage was our favorite). *55 Sunrise Point Rd. (Rte. 1), Lincolnville; 207/236-7716; sunrisepoint.com; doubles from $$.*

Portland Harbor Hotel In a town with surprisingly few worthy hotels, this is the top choice for both location (right in the Old Port) and comfort (spacious rooms are done up in butter yellow with dark-wood furnishings; granite bathrooms have outsize soaking tubs). *468 Fore St., Portland; 888/798-9090 or 207/775-9090; portlandharborhotel.com; doubles from $$.*

Yachtsman Lodge & Marina The best of the seven delightful properties run by the owners of the White Barn Inn (a roster that also includes the oceanfront Beach House Inn). The Yachtsman, on the banks of the Kennebunk River, is the most informal of the lot: a chic converted motel whose 30 airy rooms have cathedral ceilings, bead-board paneling, and French doors opening to semiprivate patios. *57 Ocean Ave., Kennebunkport; 207/967-2511; yachtsmanlodge. com; doubles from $$.*

WHERE TO EAT + SHOP FOR FOOD

Barnacle Billy's Enjoy lobster everything, not to mention a cocktail or two, on a sundeck with harbor views. *70 Perkins Cove Rd., Ogunquit; 800/866-5575 or 207/646-5575; lobster rolls and clam chowder for two ✗✗.*

Bayview Market & Takeout Local character Larry Reynolds fixes outstanding crab rolls at his roadside trailer. *28 Bayview Rd. (Rte. 175), Penobscot; 207/326-4882; crab rolls for two ✗.*

Browne Trading Market New England's finest seafood market sells incredible smoked salmon, delicacies for picnics, and more than a dozen varieties of caviar. *262 Commercial St., Portland; 207/ 775-7560; browne-trading.com.*

Chase's Daily Equal parts funky farmstead and buzzing restaurant that sells fresh produce in a former warehouse; go for the succulent heirloom tomatoes. *96 Main St., Belfast; 207/338-0555; lunch for two ✗✗.*

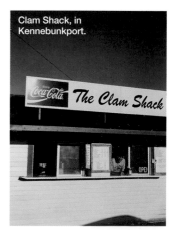

Clam Shack, in Kennebunkport.

Cinque Terre Authentically replicated Ligurian dishes an ocean away from where they originated, prepared with Maine's own meat and produce (naturally, lobster appears in the trenette pasta with summer squash). *36 Wharf St., Portland; 207/347 6154; dinner for two* ✗✗.

Clam Shack Serves what is universally accepted as Maine's best lobster roll. *2 Western Ave. (Rte. 9), Kennebunkport; 207/967-3321; lobster rolls for two* ✗✗.

Duckfat Relive childhood over panini, duck-fat-cooked fries, and fizzy root-beer floats at this homey eatery. *43 Middle St., Portland; 207/774-8080; lunch for two* ✗✗.

Five Fifty-Five One of Portland's most assured restaurants; the philosophy follows the greenmarket school of fresh, clean-flavored food, such as a mint-and-lemon-tinged pea soup laced with baby fiddleheads. *555 Congress St., Portland; 207/761-0555; dinner for two* ✗✗✗.

Five Islands Farm Fantastic selection of Maine farmstead cheeses. *1375 Five Islands Rd., Georgetown; 207/371-9383; fiveislandsfarm.com.*

Fore Street Faded, down-home charm and Maine's finest earthbound food. *288 Fore St., Portland; 207/775-2717; dinner for two* ✗✗✗.

Francine Bistro A loyal following sometimes equals long lines, but chef Brian Hill's locally sourced dishes are worth the wait. *55 Chestnut St., Camden; 207/230-0083; dinner for two* ✗✗✗.

Hugo's Former Thomas Keller disciple Rob Evans riffs on familiar dishes using regional ingredients, with masterful results. *88 Middle St., Portland; 207/774-8538; dinner for two* ✗✗✗.

Joshua's Beautifully restored 1774 clapboard house, six miles

Dessert at Primo, in Rockland.

east of chef Joshua Mather's family farm; mom Barbara is the hostess, and father Mort harvests most of the produce. The kitchen dazzles with dishes like the caramelized-onion haddock with wild-mushroom risotto. *1637 Post Rd., Wells; 207/646-3355; dinner for two* ✗✗✗.

K. Horton Specialty Foods The top Portland cheesemonger. *28 Monument Square, Portland; 207/228-2056; khortonfoods.com.*

MC Perkins Cove Coastal fare in a glassed-in space with dramatic views of tidal pools and the Atlantic beyond. *111 Perkins Cove Rd., Ogunquit; 207/646-6263; dinner for two* ✗✗.

Morse's Sauerkraut Clean, crunchy kraut at its tangy finest. *3856 Washington Rd. (Rte. 220), North Waldoboro; 866/832-5569 or 207/832-5569; lunch for two* ✗✗.

Primo Star chef Melissa Kelly's dishes are delicate yet robust, and all prepared with produce from her garden. *2 S. Main St. (Rte. 73), Rockland; 207/596-0770; dinner for two* ✗✗✗.

Red's Eats Roadside stand famous for its delicious lobster sandwich. *41 Water St. at Main St. (Rte. 1), Wiscasset; 207/882-6128; lobster rolls for two* ✗✗.

Scratch Baking Co. A menu of bagels and breads—from ciabatta to sunflower spelt—that rotates daily, along with popular morning-meal staples like smokehouse bacon and farm-fresh eggs. *416 Preble St., South Portland; 207/799-0668.*

Sewalls Orchard The best place to pick your own wild blueberries from mid- to late summer. *259 Masalin Rd., Lincolnville; 207/763-3956; sewallsorchard.com.*

Silvery Moon Creamery & Smiling Hill Farm Family owned since the 1700's and a modern-day favorite for house-made ice cream, butter, and artisanal cheeses. *781 County Rd. (Rte. 22), Westbrook; 207/775-4818; smilinghill.com.*

Standard Baking Co. Maine's best bakery is housed in an atmospheric old brick warehouse, where there's always a queue for baguettes, sourdough *boules,* and plush brioche. Secret weapon: the heavenly ginger-bread. *75 Commercial St., Portland; 207/773-2112.*

White Barn Inn A formal throwback to a more sophisticated age, with zesty food that's anything but traditional. *37 Beach Ave., Kennebunk; 207/967-2321; dinner for two* ✗✗✗✗.

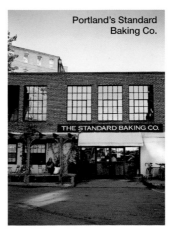

Portland's Standard Baking Co.

Best Farm-Fresh Produce

Chef Brian Hill of Francine Bistro shares his shopping list for the Camden Farmers' Market *(camden farmersmarket.org).*

Hahn's End "Cheese made by former nuclear chemist Debbie Hahn and her husband, Drew."

Half Moon Farm "Sandy and John Spinney offer tiny fava beans, 'Delfino' cilantro, perfect baby green beans, and great artisanal jams."

Hubbard Brook Farm "Kevin Weiser is the king of corn, with a different variety every week, along with luscious peaches, nectarines, and his wife's red and golden raspberries."

Maine-ly Poultry "Beautiful corn-fed and free-range chickens and eggs from John and Sheila Barnstein."

Oyster Creek Mushroom Company "Dan 'the Mushroom Man' has fresh morels in the spring, chanterelles and black trumpets in the summer, and incredible matsutakes in the fall."

KEY TO THE DINING PRICE ICONS ✗ UNDER $25 ✗✗ $25–$74 ✗✗✗ $75–$149 ✗✗✗✗ $150–$299 ✗✗✗✗✗ $300 AND UP

WHERE THERE'S SMOKE...

FROM KANSAS TO NORTH CAROLINA,
A QUEST FOR THE COUNTRY'S BEST
BARBECUE. BY MATT LEE AND TED LEE

Photographed by Marcus Nilsson

BEYOND THE GAS STATION PUMPS AND PAST THE RACKS OF HOSTESS CAKES,

a warren of tables and booths makes up the Kansas City, Kansas, barbecue joint Oklahoma Joe's. On a steamy Wednesday in July, the dean of Kansas City barbecue, Ardie Davis, sat alone in the restaurant beneath drowsy ceiling fans, looking at his watch.

When he spied us, Davis shot up from his seat, and though it was just after 11 a.m., dashed toward the cashier to place his order: sliced beef brisket, pork ribs, french fries, beans, and burnt ends.

The woman behind the counter looked up from her register. "Burnt ends ain't ready yet," she said. "Y'all gon' stick around?"

"Wonderful," Davis replied, and explained: you won't find these caramelized morsels from the edges of the brisket, where the seasoning gathers as the fat renders, on the menu, because they're only served on Wednesdays and Saturdays; in a half-hour, the lunch line would extend out the door, and then...who knows when they might run out?

Davis wasn't taking any chances. An avuncular retiree with a sturdy build and snowy hair, he's the author of five books about barbecue and has been a competition-barbecue judge for more than 25 years. Oklahoma Joe's began life on that circuit in the early 90's as the Slaughterhouse Five, a team of barbecue enthusiasts who got together to cook at weekend championships around the Midwest and the South. The team won so many awards that by 1996 they opened a restaurant. Compared with Kansas City institutions like the circa-1920 Arthur Bryant's, O.J.'s is a modern place, using state-of-the-art smokers that cook meat with a combination of natural gas and wood.

When our food arrived, Davis took a bite of the rib, which pleased him immensely. "See this bark here?" he said, pointing to a reddish-black shard of crust on the surface of the rib. "You want it crispy like that on the outside, but tender on the inside. And there," he said, pointing to a layer of almost lurid pinkness just beneath the skin that extended the length of the rib, "that's the smoke ring, the sign that it's been properly smoked. O.J.'s uses more wood than gas. You go to some places and you can't taste any smoke at all."

The ribs were, indeed, porky and redolent of white oak, and they disappeared quickly. The brisket was fall-apart tender—a tad dry, but then there were sauces to dress it with (permissible in Kansas City).

Finally, the burnt ends came, and they were wonderful: salty, glistening with smoke-tinged fat, prickly with the heat of black pepper. To us they seemed the best bit, but Davis was having none of it. "They're too salty, and there's no bark on 'em," he said, but conceded, "Concerning taste, there's no argument. That's what makes barbecue fun."

BARBECUE: A BRIEF (25 MILLENNIA) HISTORY

What is it about barbecue? Historians tell us that for 250,000 years, man has applied low, slow heat to proteins to make them meltingly succulent and delicious. Christopher Columbus discovered the Taino people of modern-day Haiti cooking fish and meats on a grate of sticks lashed together and suspended above a fire, and dousing their food with a scorching chili sauce. Portuguese and Spanish explorers in the New World found American Indians practicing a similar culinary art, and as waves of European settlers and enslaved Africans landed in North America in the 18th and 19th

OPPOSITE: Preparing pulled pork at Arthur Bryant's, a legend since the 1920's in Kansas City, Missouri. PREVIOUS SPREAD, FROM LEFT: The smoke pit at A&R Bar-B-Que, in Memphis; a table with a takeout order of beef brisket at Arthur Bryant's.

centuries, they adapted the technique to the food traditions they brought from their homelands and the raw materials of their new environment. Germans who settled in the Hill Country of Texas smoked fat pork sausages over mesquite or oak of the region. In Kansas City, a cow town at the crossroads of several important early trade routes, the abundance of pecan and hickory meant that deeply smoky beef brisket and ribs came to define the city's style. Barbecue emerged as something more than heating and seasoning protein—it became culture.

Every morsel of barbecue tells a story, starting with the meat: if it's sausage, you're in or around Austin, Texas. Mutton? Owensboro, Kentucky. Whole hog might be eastern North Carolina, western Tennessee, or upstate South Carolina, depending on which hardwoods you're using and how you seasoned your pork. Did the pit master put a dry rub of black pepper and salt on it before laying it over the coals? Did he baste it once it was on the heat, and if so, with what kind of liquid? Did he turn the pig before it was done, and did he dress it

with sauce before it was served? Every decision a contemporary pit master makes might be rooted in tradition, in the choices our ancestors made; and even today these regional differences hold up.

We'd set out on a 3,000-mile odyssey, exploring the contours of American barbecue the way hikers thrill to the changing topography of the Appalachian Trail. We were in search of the ultimate barbecue, of course, but more than that, we were on a quest to determine what perfect barbecue might mean today. We had notions of the quintessential barbecue joint: family-run (and with a few generations on-site, preferably), exuding an authentically acquired patina of age. We were fairly sure the barbecue of our dreams would come from a dwelling with a certain undersung-ness about it (and likely not a place with a punning or deliberately alliterative name, like Swineomite or Peter's Piggy Palace).

But for the sake of our journey, we set out with open minds, hungry mouths, and—did we mention?—a 1972 Buick Limited. We'd seen the ad for the gold-colored, black-vinyl-topped Limited online about a month before our departure. It only had 90,000 miles on the clock, and we watched as the asking price dropped, then dropped again as our departure date approached. About a week before we left, we sent a check for the car, sight unseen, to a guy named Mick, in Stillwell, Kansas, a suburb of Kansas City.

Why a decades-old, 6,000-pound car, when gasoline prices were running at an all-time high? Because our quest defied common sense, and we needed a vehicle to match. The Buick had compelling features beyond its 455 V-8 engine and black brocade interior. Namely, four cigarette lighters—critical because we were packing our phones, one laptop for note-taking, another for downloading photos, and a small AC car refrigerator (we'd be ordering a lot of barbecue, tasting lightly, and would want to keep samples for comparison). But more than all that, piloting the old American workhorse, demanding vast quantities of vigilance, time, and fuel, seemed to project a oneness with the 'cue.

FIRST STOP: KANSAS CITY

It was at the airport that we learned Kansas City lives and breathes barbecue the way New Orleans does gumbo. We'd simply asked the man behind the rental-car counter what his favorite barbecue spot was. "Gates, definitely Gates. Best burnt ends—you'll want the mixed plate, too, with fries," he said. Then a coworker chimed in. "Naw, meat's too fatty at Gates," he said. "Okie Joe's is the place. The sauce is spicier there, too."

Everywhere we went in Kansas City, we ran into barbecue. As we fired up the Buick, tightening a loose hose clamp, we watched Mick's neighbor Larry load coolers into an SUV, headed to Peculiar, Missouri, to compete in "the Peculiar BBQ Roundup." Our session with Ardie Davis at Oklahoma Joe's was a superb first impression, but it wasn't until we rolled into the parking lot at Arthur Bryant's and saw the mountain of cordwood just beyond the kitchen's back door and the chuffing smokestack that we realized there was an element missing from our O.J.'s experience: the process.

Inside Arthur Bryant's, a snaking line stretched to the door, and as we inched toward the order window, an opening in a Plexiglas wall, we watched, riveted, as the workers performed the rough-and-tumble procedure: pulling a whole brisket, blackened and quivering, from the white-enameled brick smoker; throwing down a broad sheet of red butcher paper; slapping on it a few slices of Wonder bread followed by a generous heaping of brisket

WE SET OUT ON A 3,000-MILE ODYSSEY, EXPLORING THE CONTOURS OF AMERICAN BARBECUE THE WAY HIKERS THRILL TO THE CHANGING TOPOGRAPHY OF THE APPALACHIAN TRAIL

ribbons; piling a fistful of steaming, thick-cut fries on top; then rolling the heaping mass into a package the size of a swaddled newborn.

In the fundamentals of pit cookery, Arthur Bryant's shone: brisket beautifully marbled, lightly smoky; pork ribs perfectly moist, not too salty; the sauce, rust-colored, almost gritty with dried spices, with a delectable Worcestershire-coriander inflection and a snappy vinegar bite. But since the taste, the texture, the flavor is so tied to a sense of place, it stands to reason that the way the establishment envelops you in the process—and its past—matters.

SNOOTS AND WHOLE HOG

We've heard all the old saws on the subject: Barbecue is like sex—tough to describe, you just know it when it's good. Barbecue is religion, people say, to explain the rectitudinous fervor that regional styles tend to engender. And we've met leagues of barbecue one-upmen from Charleston to Charlottesville, Brooklyn to Laurel Canyon.

All that bluster, all that talk—it doesn't do much to elucidate the experience of traveling through a place, eating great barbecue. In St. Louis, we bought the region's specialties, snoots—no pretty way around it, it's the snout of a hog—from C & K, a takeout window with nary a wood chip in sight, but a steady stream of locals on a lazy Sunday. We took the platter to the park below the Gateway Arch, near where the Mississippi River had submerged the river walk. Like oversize pork rinds, with the texture of a rice cake, the snoots were sluiced with a tomatoey sauce that had the right amount of sweetness and heat cutting through its deeply porky hit. Did we get too wrapped up in

OPPOSITE, FROM LEFT: Jerry's owner, Jerry Bland, at his restaurant in Parsons, Tennessee; a takeout order of beef brisket sandwich on Wonder bread with fries wrapped in butcher paper at Arthur Bryant's.

it all—the newness of the snout, the majesty of the arch, and the fear of the rising river drowning the old Buick? Whatever the case, we loved the snoots, and we ate every last bite.

And it was an altogether different kind of love from the intoxicating one we experienced when we dropped down to Nashville and Memphis, Tennessee. In the space of two days, we hit Charlie Vergos's Rendezvous, Neely's, Central, Leonard's, Tops, and Cozy Corner—a charry, sticky blur of ribs and even more ribs, with only a trip to the Stax Museum of American Soul Music for respite. We were worried the resulting hangover might color our experience of the more fragile whole-hog tradition that lingers on in the counties east of Memphis, near Lexington, Tennessee.

No chance. About halfway to Nashville, we were hunting for a barbecue restaurant among the grain mills and goat farms of Route 69 when a freshly painted barn-red hut came into view, a plume of smoke issuing from somewhere behind the building. A line of customers queued outdoors by a screened window. By this point in the trip, we

knew what we had to do. We ordered our pulled-pork sandwiches, lightly sauced, and made our way to the perfunctory dining room, which is more like a freestanding screened-in porch. A truck out back was filled with squared hickory rods—evidently there's a drumstick mill in the area that sells the curved or split blanks, the rejects, to the local barbecue shops to burn. In a barrel nearby a few bushels of sticks were crackling into the swelter of summer afternoon. Once the fire settled down, the glowing embers would be shoveled into the smoker to gently cook the pigs. The pulled-pork sandwich at Jerry's Bar-B-Que was outstanding, expertly seasoned and lubricated, plenty smoky, with a chunky house-cut slaw on top for tonic balance and a sauce that hinted at spice without overstating the obvious.

We were beginning to spot a pattern with the barbecue joints we liked most, a certain disrespect for the boundaries between indoors and outdoors, kitchen and dining room, a fundamental flexibility that allows for the main ingredients—smoke and fat—to flow where they may. Customers get to see

the action firsthand and inhale a strong whiff of the wares. In a roadside setting, selling a product as slippery as barbecue, an open kitchen is an expression of honesty.

SKIP THE SALAD, THIS IS BARBECUE

One thousand miles into our journey, we resolved that perfect barbecue is a liberation from restaurant conventions. It knows no appetizers or white tablecloths. As we rolled across North Carolina, we categorized the fresh-air, order-window type places that use hardwoods from the local forests and specialize in one style of barbecue as Heritage. And the chains we had encountered? Those with air-conditioning, the hi-may-I-help-you waitstaff, the all-things-to-all-people menu and wines by the glass, we dubbed Contemporary.

But in Raleigh we found a third barbecue style—Postmodern—at the Pit. Eyes rolled and tongues wagged in this town when developer Greg Hatem, a guy with a knack for restoring downtown landmarks and outfitting them with upscale restaurants, recruited one of eastern North Carolina's preeminent old-school whole-hog pit masters, Ed Mitchell, to take up shop in a loftlike former meatpacking warehouse (for comparison's sake, imagine your local morning show luring the Rolling Stones to be the house band). Though Mitchell still wears his trademark overalls, the place is a barbecue joint for a new age: the kitchen is a spotless, open, stainless-steel affair at the back of a dining room with—you guessed it!—white tablecloths. All the meats—and, one presumes, the fish and barbecued tofu—are organic, humanely raised specimens.

We chose to sit in the stylish bar area, where college guys drink Bud Light longnecks, gnaw on ribs, and watch The Game on big-screen TV's. And while Mitchell's briquette-fired smokers might raise a few eyebrows farther east in the state, we were impressed by the chopped whole hog, which was classically eastern N.C. in style, with a blast of vinegar, red pepper flakes, and smoke, and the baby back ribs, with the lightest brush of caramelized sauce to frame the background smoke and salt. And they were crispy outside and moist inside. There were some thoughtful regional

FROM FAR LEFT: Lexington Barbecue, in North Carolina; baby back ribs, chopped pork, and beef brisket with baked beans and mac and cheese at the Pit, in Raleigh, North Carolina; Ed Mitchell, owner of the Pit; the dining room at Wilber's Barbecue, in Goldsboro, North Carolina.

touches up front we didn't expect, like a delicious sangria made from North Carolina Scupperdine wine. We had a lovely dinner at the Pit, but the place got us thinking: At what point does barbecue become so mannered it stops being barbecue?

WILBER'S: BARBECUE NIRVANA?

The following morning, we set out east before the crack of dawn. We'd read—and confirmed over the phone—that Wilber's Barbecue, in Goldsboro, North Carolina, opens at 6 a.m., and when we rumbled off the highway and into the parking lot of the sprawling roadhouse at exactly 7 o'clock, three dozen cars had already crowded the lot. Smoke puffed from a fire somewhere and lost itself in the morning's mist. We took a seat in one of the knotty-pine-paneled rooms, with wooden schoolhouse chairs and red-checked tablecloths, next to steely-haired farmers having their morning smokes and trading portentous outcomes.

"I'll tell you what," one of the men piped up. "The rain comes, there'll be a lotta IOU's going down that river." In the silence that followed, heads nodded, cigarettes got stubbed out.

Our own bleak future seemed foretold when the waitress arrived and said we could order anything we liked off the breakfast menu, but that the hogs simply weren't done cooking. Barbecue wouldn't be available until about 10.

We ordered a breakfast—brains and eggs; country ham; grits—that might have been cause to rejoice in other circumstances, but we ate them in silence. There was a long drive home ahead, and the week's worth of work to catch up on. We really didn't have a few hours to kill, but then—what's a few hours, for the perfect barbecue?

We strode back to the Buick to take stock—still not sure whether we'd be killing time here, or heading home—when we heard a voice behind us: "Hey, aren't y'all the Lee brothers?" The man juggled a Bible and a set of car keys, then set his Bible on the trunk of the car. "I don't believe it," he said. "Celebrities right here in Wilber's parking lot. I'm Willis Underwood."

We were speechless, not only because he'd mistaken two freelance writers for celebrities, but because we'd just been thinking Wilber's barbecue was the celebrity and we were the supplicants, waiting outside the trailer for a glimpse.

"Have you met Dennis? Have you been 'round back?" Underwood asked, then beckoned, "Come on!" He lit out past a fence shielding the operation from the parking lot and introduced us to Dennis Monk, who poked at the remains of a log fire that had burned down to glowing coals. A mountain of wood piled at the edge of the adjoining cornfield would last through the weekend, he said, and then they'd get another full trailerload on Monday, and a week of barbecue would begin again.

Monk shoveled up some embers from the fire and ushered us through a screen door into a brick shed about three times longer than it is wide, lit by a string of bulbs, with the smoky-sweet smell of roasting pork fat everywhere. Each of the pits—troughs, really, about waist-high, running parallel to one another down the length of each wall—held a few hogs. Walking the aisle between the troughs, he shoveled fresh coals into the bottom of the pits through openings in the wall beneath each pig.

Monk lifted a battered sheet of tin loosely covering one pig, pulled at a couple ribs, which gave readily, with a plug of meat still attached, and proffered them. "This one's about done," he said, but there was one that had already come off the pit, and was in fact being pulled inside the kitchen, did we want to see?

Leamon Park, a 35-year veteran cook at Wilber's Barbecue, was upending a bus pan full of freshly pulled pork morsels onto his board, and with two huge cleavers, hacked at it in a rhythmic round-house, chopping it down to size. He paused to season the meat with salt and pepper, and then poured what seemed like a gallon of crushed red pepper–spiced vinegar from a stainless-steel pitcher over it. Park tossed the meat with his cleavers, and the pork readily absorbed the liquid.

We ordered and left Monk to finish cooking—there were many more hogs to come off the pit, and much chopping to do before the lunchtime rush. The sandwiches were undoubtedly the best of the pilgrimage, freshly warmed, well seasoned. And by that time, Underwood's friend had showed up in his '71 fire-engine red Gran Sport convertible, and Underwood's wife and sister had arrived, too. So we all piled into the caravan of vintage Buicks, and we were on to the next place, for another bite of ethereal whole hog.

OPPOSITE: Veteran cook Leamon Park at Wilber's Barbecue.

BARBECUE GLOSSARY

BARK The charry, brown-black crust that forms on the surface of any cut of barbecue—from ribs and brisket to shoulders—that's often dry-rubbed with seasonings.

BURNT ENDS Crusty, browned morsels from the thinner ends of a brisket. Diced or chopped, they can be served alone or in a sandwich.

DIP In Owensboro, Kentucky, a mixture of Worcestershire, broth or water, and sometimes lemon or tomato juice that gets basted on mutton or is used as a seasoning.

MIDDLINGS The meat on the outside of the ribs, which is especially tender and moist.

OUTSIDE BROWN MEAT In North Carolina, this is the exposed flesh of the pig, typically the shoulder, that becomes well browned and deeply seasoned. Request it either chopped or sliced.

SHORT END On a slab of pork ribs, this is the part of the rack that tapers. It's the meatier half (and usually more expensive).

SNOOTS In St. Louis, this refers to the face and cheeks of a pig, cooked until the skin is crispy. It is typically sauced, then eaten with rib tips or in a sandwich.

WHOLE HOG A style of barbecue in which an entire pig is cooked in a pit, a process which typically takes 12 to 18 hours.

Blackberry Farm, in Walland, Tennessee.

WHEN TO GO
Fall—when the air has a slight chill and the pit masters have returned from their summer vacations—is a great time to plan a barbecue road trip.

WHERE TO STAY
KANSAS
Back N Thyme On the outskirts of Kansas City, a small-town B&B with a wraparound veranda. *1100 S. 130th St., Bonner Springs; 913/422-5207; backnthyme.com; doubles from $.*

KENTUCKY
Victorian Quarters B&B Restored Italianate mansion overlooking the Ohio River. *109 Clay St., Henderson; 270/831-2778; victorianquartersbb.com; doubles from $.*

MISSOURI
Hilton St. Louis Downtown Housed in an 1888 former bank, steps from the iconic Gateway Arch. *400 Olive St., St. Louis; 800/445-8667 or 314/436-0002; hilton.com; doubles from $.*

Raphael Hotel Grand old institution overlooking Country Club Plaza, the first suburban shopping center in the U.S. *325 Ward Pkwy., Kansas City; 800/821-5343 or 816/756-3800; raphaelkc.com; doubles from $.*

NORTH CAROLINA
Sheraton Raleigh Recently renovated 353-room property. *421 S. Salisbury St., Raleigh; 800/325-3535 or 919/834-9900; sheraton.com; doubles from $$.*

TENNESSEE
Blackberry Farm Ultra-luxe resort in the Smoky Mountains with an outstanding culinary program. *1471 W. Millers Cove Rd., Walland; 800/648-4252 or 865/984-8166; blackberryfarm. com; doubles from $$$$, including meals.*

Madison Hotel A quiet Art Deco lobby, a private rooftop bar, and 110 tastefully designed rooms. *79 Madison Ave., Memphis; 901/333-1200; madisonhotelmemphis.com; doubles from $$.*

Union Station, A Wyndham Historic Hotel Located in a former train station, with whimsically decorated interiors. *1001 Broadway, Nashville; 877/999-3223 or 615/726-1001; wyndham.com; doubles from $$.*

WHERE TO EAT
ILLINOIS
17th Street Bar & Grill Few pit masters have achieved the level of celebrity of Mike Mills, whose postmodern barn provides a range of regional styles. *1711 W. Hwy. 50, O'Fallon; 618/622-1717; dinner for two ✗✗.*

KANSAS
Oklahoma Joe's Known for its state-of-the-art smokers, which use a combo of natural gas and wood. *3002 W. 47th Ave., Kansas City; 913/722-3366; dinner for two ✗.*

KENTUCKY
Moonlite Bar-B-Q Inn The apotheosis of Owensboro's microregional mutton 'cue. Order it sliced and chopped—always with "dip"—and in a meaty burgoo (a rustic Kentucky stew). *2840 W. Parrish Ave., Owensboro; 270/684-8143; dinner for two ✗✗.*

MISSOURI
Arthur Bryant's Circa-1920's institution serving up beautifully marbled brisket on slices of Wonder bread, piled with a fistful of thick-cut fries and rolled in broad sheets of butcher paper to go. *1727 Brooklyn Ave., Kansas City; 816/231-1123; dinner for two ✗✗.*

Interior of the Pit, in Raleigh, North Carolina.

KEY TO THE HOTEL PRICE ICONS $ UNDER $250 $$ $250–$499 $$$ $500–$749 $$$$ $750–$999 $$$$$ $1,000 AND UP

Stax Museum, Memphis.

C & K Order the region's specialty, snoots, at this takeout window frequented by a steady stream of locals. *4390 Jennings Station Rd., St. Louis; 314/385-8100; dinner for two* ✘.

Gates Bar-B-Q Excellent burnt ends, mixed plate, and fries. *1221 Brooklyn Ave., Kansas City; 816/483-3880; lunch for two* ✘.

Roper's Ribs The top spot for the Gateway City's barbecue specialties, such as St. Louis–cut pork ribs, snoots, and rib tips. *6929 W. Florissant Ave., St. Louis; 314/381-6200; lunch for two* ✘✘.

NORTH CAROLINA

Lexington Barbecue Located in the self-professed world capital of barbecue, an establishment where pulled pork is the star. *Hwy. 29–70 S., Lexington; 336/249-9814; dinner for two* ✘.

The Pit A barbecue joint for a new age: organic, humanely raised meats, and a stainless-steel kitchen (manned by whole-hog pit master Ed Mitchell) at the back of a dining room with white tablecloths. *328 W. Davie St., Raleigh; 919/890-4500; dinner for two* ✘✘.

Scott's Famous Barbecue Local legend Martel Scott Jr. serves lunch in a 1960's dining room on Thursdays and Fridays. *1201 N. William St., Goldsboro; 919/734-0711; lunch for two* ✘.

Wilber's Barbecue Down-home mecca that opens at 6 a.m. for country ham, breakfast brains and eggs, and grits. *4172 U.S. Hwy. 70 E., Goldsboro; 919/778-5218; lunch for two* ✘.

TENNESSEE

A&R Bar-B-Que The rib-tip sandwich here is moist, with lingering smoke, and all too easy to eat. *1802 Elvis Presley Blvd., Memphis; 901/774-4747; lunch for two* ✘.

A rib-tip sandwich at A&R Bar-B-Que.

Central BBQ Possibly the best ribs in the area. *2249 Central Ave., Memphis; 901/272-9377; dinner for two* ✘✘.

Charlie Vergos's Rendezvous Memphis institution with an open kitchen, tucked away in an alley behind Second Street. *52 S. Second St., Memphis; 901/523-2746; dinner for two* ✘✘.

Cozy Corner Family-run spot with outstanding sliced pork shoulder, barbecued spaghetti, and the house favorite, barbecued bologna. *745 N. Parkway, Memphis; 901/527-9158; dinner for two* ✘.

Jack's Bar-B-Que Located in the thick of honky-tonk bars on Music City's tourist strip; draws local rockabilly kids and alt-country scenesters for remarkable beef brisket, pork ribs, and smoked chicken. *416 Broadway, Nashville; 615/254-5715; dinner for two* ✘.

Jerry's Bar-B-Que Outstanding pulled-pork sandwiches served with a chunky house-made slaw. *14 E. Holley St., Parsons; 731/847-7714; dinner for two* ✘.

Leonard's Pit Barbecue Pile your plate at the venerable 88-year-old establishment's lunch buffet. *5465 Fox Plaza Dr., Memphis; 901/360-1963; lunch for two* ✘.

Mary's Old Fashioned Pit Barbecue Locals line up for a superb rendition of chopped pork on a bun, as well as excellent grilled short ribs. *1108 Jefferson St., Nashville; 615/256-7696; dinner for two* ✘.

Neely's Bar-B-Que Authentic Memphis-style 'cue, with three locations across the state. *5700 Mt. Moriah, Memphis, and other locations; 901/795-4177; dinner for two* ✘✘.

Scott's Bar-B-Que Smoke rings are evident in these perfect pulled-pork sandwiches, which are topped with carrot-flecked slaw and suffused with a medium-hot sauce. *10880 Hwy. 412 W., Lexington; 731/968-0420; dinner for two* ✘.

Siler's Old-Time Bar-B-Que The most recent in a succession of joints cooking whole hogs on this site. Ask for rib meat, pit meat, or tenderloin, if you prefer. *6060 State Rte. 100 E., Henderson; 731/989-2242; lunch for two* ✘.

Tops Bar-B-Q Stellar slow-cooked-barbecue chain with 14 outposts. *1286 Union Ave., Memphis, and other locations; topsbarbq.com; lunch for two* ✘.

BRING IT BACK
Kentucky's Ale-8-One ($3) is a smooth, easy-drinking ginger ale that's a great mixer, too.

A&R Bar-B-Que, in Memphis, Tennessee.

Five Attractions Along the Way

American Kennel Club Museum of the Dog More than 700 works of art depicting man's best friend. *1721 S. Mason Rd., St. Louis; 314/821-3647; museumofthedog.org.*

International Bluegrass Music Museum Exhibits devoted to the history and legendary perfomers of Kentucky's official state music. *117 Daviess St., Owensboro, Ky.; 888/692-2656; bluegrassmuseum.org.*

North Carolina Museum of Art A light-filled complex of galleries, surrounded by gardens and pools, is the centerpiece of the recently opened expansion. *2110 Blue Ridge Rd., Raleigh, N.C.; 919/839-6262; ncartmuseum.org.*

O'Fallon Veterans' Monument Tribute to local veterans at a park with a pond and fountains. *E. Wesley Dr., O'Fallon, Ill.; ofallonveterans monument.org.*

Stax Museum of American Soul Music Located on the original site of Stax Records, which launched the careers of soul greats Isaac Hayes and Otis Redding, among others. *926 E. McLemore Ave., Memphis; 901/946-2535; staxmuseum.com.*

KEY TO THE DINING PRICE ICONS ✘ UNDER $25 ✘✘ $25–$74 ✘✘✘ $75–$149 ✘✘✘✘ $150–$299 ✘✘✘✘✘ $300 AND UP

Photographed by Thayer Allyson Gowdy

THE ALLURE OF MARIN

ALONG HIGHWAY 1 NORTH OF SAN FRANCISCO LIES A FOODIE ENCLAVE WITH LEISURELY HIKES, TRANQUIL PICNIC SPOTS, AND A CASUAL CALIFORNIA VIBE. BY OLIVER STRAND

IT'S JUST A 35-MILE DRIVE FROM THE GOLDEN Gate Bridge to Point Reyes Station. The distance is pocket change by California's sprawling standards, but the trip takes forever—or to be fair, a little more than an hour—because the best way to get there is on Highway 1, a narrow ribbon of asphalt that twists along sheer coastal cliffs before plunging past Stinson Beach and finally jagging through Point Reyes Station, a dusty little town that's outwardly unchanged from a century ago.

Point Reyes Station is the unofficial seat of West Marin, which, in turn, is the unofficial name for the hardscrabble coastal part of Marin County. It's one of the most unspoiled corners of the state, a region that has more in common with the sun-faded, handmade California of the 1970's than the wealthy nearby suburbs of Mill Valley and Sausalito.

Which isn't to say West Marin isn't welcoming, or even luxurious—to judge by the plush comforters at Manka's Inverness Lodge, a collection of meticulously decorated cabins scattered along a wooded hillside. Whether you consider it appealing depends on what you expect from northern California. You won't find $1,000 bottles of wine or a state-of-the-art spa. But if you want to pick up line-caught albacore tuna salad at the deli, go for a four-hour hike in a wild-elk reserve, or take in the sunset while throwing back a few dozen oysters harvested that morning from the estuary where Sir Francis

Drake ran aground in 1579, that's easy. And there's the driving: the distances within West Marin are short, the roads are windy but smooth, and you're always skimming along a nature preserve, the coast, or a picture-book farm. Here, my wife and I found, even running out to grab lunch can be an automotive pleasure.

I first started exploring West Marin more than 15 years ago, when I was a student at the University of California, Berkeley, and I traversed every corner of the Bay Area in my battered Honda Accord. When I returned this time, it was for the food and wine: Cowgirl Creamery's cheeses, Sean Thackrey's legendary Rhône-style reds, the grass-fed beef of Marin Sun Farms, oysters fresh from Tomales Bay. It's a remarkable showing, even for a gustatory state like California, and more impressive still when you consider that the largest town around here has about 500 residents, and that much of the land in the area is a part of Point Reyes National Seashore, a 71,000-acre reserve.

Geologically speaking, Point Reyes is basically a mountainous stretch of Big Sur that migrated up the coast. The earth, always unusually active in California, is still rearranging West Marin: the land has been grinding northward for thousands of years, lurching a full 20 feet during the San Francisco earthquake of 1906. (One inch every six months is average.) But the San Andreas Fault

OPPOSITE: Point Reyes National Seashore, as seen from the cliffs above its lighthouse.

TOP, FROM LEFT: The famed barbecued bivalves at Marshall Store Oyster Bar; a view from the boathouse at Manka's Inverness Lodge; artisanal cheeses at Cowgirl Creamery, in Point Reyes Station. BELOW: Outside Nick's Cove & Cottages, in Marshall.

I'M SEDUCED BY THE SIMPLICITY OF EATING IN CALIFORNIA—WHERE EVEN THE MOST SOPHISTICATED, SATISFYING MEALS CAN FEEL EFFORTLESS

doesn't feel sinister here. The rift valley is lush and shady, California folded up on itself.

We were staying at Manka's, in Inverness, where the cabins are so peaceful they have an almost narcotic effect. The main lodge and its legendary restaurant burned to the ground in 2006, so we made the 15-minute drive to Point Reyes Station to grab lunch. Our plan was to go to Cowgirl Cantina—a deli counter opened by Cowgirl Creamery—and put together a picnic for a hike through the national seashore. But first we couldn't help lingering at the farmers' market that sets up next to Toby's Feed Barn on Saturday mornings, sipping expertly made cappuccinos from the unassuming coffee stall, buying sackfuls of organic apples, and sharing a braised-goat sandwich.

The converted barn that houses Cowgirl Creamery & Cantina is just a block off Highway 1. There's an impressive cheese shop, and you can spy some cheese making through plate-glass windows, but we were there to stock up for our hike. We chose from house-cured gravlax, fig-and-blue-cheese salad, seared day-boat tuna with fennel, assorted Fra' Mani charcuterie, duck pâté, and still-warm bread from Brick Maiden. We also picked up a bottle of a floral Pinot Noir from Pey-Marin, one of the more promising local wineries, and a piece of Pierce Pt., a Muscat-washed whole-milk cheese rolled in dried herbs. There was more to the menu, which changes daily, but my daypack had only so much room.

There's no way to see all of Point Reyes National Seashore in one day. An elk preserve is located to

the north; steep peaks are covered with pines to the south; coastal highlands are blanketed with brush. Then there are the roads to the ocean through a lunar landscape of rolling hills and active pasture. We decided to start at the southern end and loop down to the Pacific. For four hours we experienced what passes for paradise when you spend most of the year overworked in a busy metropolis: we didn't encounter another human. Instead, we came across fallow deer, river otters, and a turkey vulture standing with outstretched wings. When we sat down for our picnic, we looked out on the ocean and, as if on cue, a school of gray whales appeared, migrating south.

A roadside sign at Nick's Cove & Cottages, below.

MOST OF CALIFORNIA'S SHORELINE IS TOO rugged to enjoy up close. Which is why Tomales Bay—a long, shallow body of water formed where the San Andreas Fault dips under the Pacific Ocean—is such a pleasant oddity. I also have a culinary affection for the gentle bay: fed by freshwater streams and open to the ocean, it's where the finest oysters in the state are grown.

Many of the oyster farms are clustered around Marshall, a snaking 20-minute drive north of Point Reyes Station. The most famous of them, Hog Island Oyster Company, sells unshucked oysters—but charges $5 per person ($8 on weekends) for a spot at a picnic table. Our next stop was Tomales Bay Oyster Company, a few miles south, where jumbo oysters are $16 for the dozen, seats at the tables don't cost a penny, and the weekend crowds make it feel like a bivalve Coachella.

But at the Marshall Store & Oyster Bar, a seafood shack perched on timber pylons, we found a dining experience that's even more low-key, the ultimate example of a certain kind of meal: unfussy, delicious, relaxed. It's nominally a general

Toby's Feed Barn, in Point Reyes Station, above. OPPOSITE: Harvesting bivalves at Tomales Bay Oyster Company, in Marshall.

store, and though they sell beer and wine—including some inspired selections from importer Kermit Lynch—they can't legally serve it, though they will lend you a corkscrew. The store farms its own exquisite oysters, and prepares them four ways: raw, Rockefeller (piled with spinach and cheese), barbecued (grilled with house-made barbecue sauce), or, its newest specialty, chorizo and buttered (cooked with Mexican sausage). We happily ordered a mix of a few dozen and carried them out to a barrel on the narrow strip of land between Highway 1 and the bay, where we drank a crisp Sancerre from paper cups.

I'm seduced by the simplicity of eating in California. It's a place where even the most sophisticated and satisfying meals can feel easy, almost effortless. But when Christine and I ate at Nick's Cove & Cottages, a small hotel in Marshall where rooms are converted fishermen's shacks, the food felt unnecessarily complicated. And while we enjoyed our meal at Olema Inn & Restaurant, set in a 100-year-old clapboard building, the night we were there the dining room was so loud we couldn't hold a conversation.

So for our final evening we made reservations at Drakes Beach Café. It's part of an oceanfront visitor's center, an architectural flashback for those of us who went on school field trips during the Carter administration (wood beams; fliers pinned to corkboard), and three years ago it started serving candlelit prix fixe dinners on weekends. It welcomes BYO, and we brought a bottle of Orion, a blend from Sean Thackrey, the cult winemaker.

The dinner was heartfelt and idiosyncratic; Slow Food cuisine served in a snack bar. And because it was so intimate, it felt romantic. It wasn't until we left the café and walked through the bracing night air to our car, the surf crashing a few feet away, that we realized how isolated we were. San Francisco may have been just a few miles down the coast, but the stars that filled the sky above us seemed closer.

A hiking trail in Point Reyes National Seashore.

roadhouse, specializes in local seafood. *23240 Hwy. 1, Marshall; 866/636-4257 or 415/663-1033; nickscove.com; doubles from $$, including breakfast; dinner for two ✖✖✖.*

Olema Druids Hall Four-suite inn in a converted 1885 meeting hall, with a rambling, charmingly overgrown garden. *9870 Shoreline, Hwy. 1, Olema; 866/554-4255 or 415/663-8727; olemadruidshall. com; doubles from $, including breakfast.*

Olema Inn & Restaurant A former saloon and later inn from Olema's livelier boomtown days, this 124-year-old clapboard hotel has six guest rooms furnished with tasteful country antiques. *10000 Sir Francis Drake Blvd., Olema; 415/663-9559; theolemainn.com; doubles from $, including breakfast.*

WHEN TO GO
Located 35 miles from the Golden Gate Bridge, West Marin is at its best in fall and spring, when the days are sunny and temperate. The nights are cool year-round, and Point Reyes National Seashore is often misty. A long weekend gives you plenty of time to explore the coast.

WHERE TO STAY
Manka's Inverness Lodge Rustic collection of meticulously decorated cabins whose Americana-inspired interiors include plush, plaid-upholstered couches, beds made from tree limbs, vintage tubs, and roaring stone fireplaces. *30 Callendar Way, Inverness; 415/669-1034; mankas.com; doubles from $$, including breakfast.*

Nick's Cove & Cottages Twelve luxuriously appointed former fishermen's shacks, some with private decks overlooking Tomales Bay. The restaurant, a historic

WHERE TO EAT + SHOP
Cowgirl Creamery & Cantina One block off Highway 1, this converted barn now houses the region's most impressive artisanal cheeses; the accompanying cantina serves the perfect picnic provisions. *80 Fourth St., Point Reyes Station; 415/663-9335; picnic lunch for two ✖.*

Drakes Bay Oyster Farms For brinier bivalves than those harvested in Tomales Bay, head to Point Reyes National Seashore, where oysters are exposed to the cold Pacific waters. *17171 Sir Francis Drake Blvd., Inverness; 415/669-1149; drakesbayfamily farms.com; dozen oysters ✖.*

Drakes Beach Café Enjoy Slow Food by candlelight in this charming 1970's-era throwback. *1 Drakes Beach Rd., Inverness; 415/669-1297; prix fixe dinner for two ✖✖✖.*

Hog Island Oyster Company The most celebrated of Marshall's oyster farms, serving unshucked bivalves and offering no-frills outdoor seating (book in advance for weekends). *20215 Rte. 1, Marshall; 415/663-9218; dozen oysters ✖, table charge from $5 per person.*

Marshall Store & Oyster Bar Four styles of oysters—raw, Rockefeller, barbecued, or chorizo-buttered—served in an unfussy seafood shack disguised as an even more unfussy general store. *19225 Hwy. 1, Marshall; 415/663-1339; lunch for two ✖✖.*

Toby's Feed Barn Charming little all-purpose gathering spot in a converted barn in downtown Point Reyes Station. For sale: dried fruits and nuts, tasteful jams, and bulk items; there's also an espresso bar, an art gallery, a homey events space, and even a room in the back for yoga classes. The Saturday farmers' market sets up right next door. *11250 Hwy. 1, Point Reyes Station; 415/663-1223.*

Tomales Bay Oyster Company The oldest continuously run shellfish farm in California; picnic tables overlooking the water are first come, first served. *15479 Hwy. 1, Marshall; 415/663-1242; dozen oysters ✖.*

WHAT TO SEE + DO
Point Reyes National Seashore Seventy-one thousand acres of coastal wilderness protected by the National Park Service, with dramatic windswept beaches, an elk preserve, a lighthouse that's open for tours, and some of the loveliest hiking trails in northern California. *1 Bear Valley Rd., Point Reyes Station; 415/464-5100; nps.gov/pore.*

Room 3 at Olema Druids Hall.

KEY TO THE HOTEL PRICE ICONS $ UNDER $250 $$ $250–$499 $$$ $500–$749 $$$$ $750–$999 $$$$$ $1,000 AND UP
KEY TO THE DINING PRICE ICONS ✖ UNDER $25   ✖✖ $25–$74   ✖✖✖ $75–$149   ✖✖✖✖ $150–$299   ✖✖✖✖✖ $300 AND UP

Savoring the specialty of the house at the Marshall Store & Oyster Bar.

Top Four Picnic Spots

Cowgirl Creamery cofounder Sue Conley shares her favorite places for a meal outdoors.

Abbott's Lagoon, Point Reyes National Seashore "A gentle one-and-a-half-mile hike onto bright white sand dunes above the ocean." *Access the trailhead via a no-fee dirt parking lot just off Pierce Point Road; nps.gov/pore.*

Arch Rock, Point Reyes National Seashore "An easy eight-mile roundtrip hike from the visitors' center to a glorious rock outcropping overlooking the Pacific." *At the end of the Bear Valley Trail; nps.gov/pore.*

Inspiration Point at Heart's Desire Beach, Tomales Bay State Park "It's just a short walk from the parking lot to a clearing with views of the bay." *Drive north along Pierce Point Road to the park, then turn right and descend to Heart's Desire Beach; tomalesbay.net.*

Redwood Grove Picnic Area, Samuel P. Taylor State Park "Located alongside Lagunitas Creek, where salmon spawn after the first autumn rainfall." *8899 Sir Francis Drake Blvd., Lagunitas; parks.ca.gov.*

AMERICA'S LATEST VINTAGE

IN THE SLEEPY SOUTHEASTERN CORNER OF
WASHINGTON STATE, A QUIET REVOLUTION IS UNDER
WAY. MEET SOME OF THE PASSIONATE—SOME WOULD
SAY OBSESSED—VINTNERS, CHEFS, AND FARMERS
WHO ARE MAKING WALLA WALLA THIS COUNTRY'S NEXT
GREAT WINE DESTINATION. BY BRUCE SCHOENFELD

Photographed by João-Ganziani

I WON'T SOON FORGET THE VERY FIRST MEAL I ATE IN WALLA WALLA.

It was 11 years ago, just as the local wine industry was beginning to boom. One of the area's leading viticulturists, a man of some sophistication, took me to what he pointedly called "the best restaurant in town." His quote marks hung in the air like smoke; before long, I understood why. The restaurant was a family steak house, on the model of a Sizzler but lacking the predictability of a chain. The room smelled like a school cafeteria, and the meat that arrived at our table tasted like something an office-supply store might sell.

Now you can sit at a table in Dayton, Washington, half an hour outside Walla Walla, and revel in the scent of just-picked basil. Out here in the country where Lewis and Clark waited out a winter by eating horses, owners Mae Schrey and Anne Jaso and their kitchen staff at the Weinhard Café serve up caramelized-sweet-onion tarts, pan-seared scallops, and pies that range from pecan bourbon to raspberry rhubarb. Things have come a long way from the days of the office-supply steak.

There's an often told story, which I heard three times in less than a week, that back in the late 1800's Walla Walla chose to be the site of the new penitentiary instead of the state capital. Local historians dismiss it as apocryphal, but it might as well be true. Until quite recently, this city of 33,000 appears to have taken pains to deflect the attention brought by its humorously euphonious name, doing little to lure visitors and exhibiting a profound suspicion toward the unfamiliar. The wheat farmers who made up the bulk of the population were satisfied to live out lives as dry and monochromatic as the crop that paid their bills, set against a faceless panorama of grain elevators, chain motels, and squat, bungalow-style houses. Even today, Walla Walla seems to have been dropped onto this corner of the southeastern Washington prairie by sheer happenstance. (The Columbia River flows nearby but plays no role in the city's geography.) Most of downtown is still filled with buildings that look more small-town Texas than Pacific Northwest. Venture off Main Street and you're on the set of *The Last Picture Show*.

Yet lately, life in Walla Walla has been transformed by the wine industry. Some of America's best vintages are currently being made in Walla Walla, which couldn't boast of a single commercially viable grapevine a quarter-century ago. Even as late as 1990, when tumbleweeds blew through an all-but-abandoned Main Street, only five wineries were operating here. By 2009, there were more than a hundred in the region, producing the requisite Cabernet Sauvignon, Chardonnay, and Merlot, but also redefining the area with Syrah and Sémillon.

The new tasting rooms that sprout from the wheat fields every month, making architectural statements with their obtuse angles and walls of glass, are attracting carloads of wine adventurers who stumble across a coveted bottle and then set out for the viticultural frontier for a weekend of tasting. The infusion of money, combined with a spirit of entrepreneurial enthusiasm, has helped remake the town. Restaurants aren't the only manifestation of the new Walla Walla: the art scene is growing (artist Jim Dine casts his works, including one on display at the Guggenheim Bilbao, at the Walla Walla Foundry), and boutique businesses—from the organic farm and the *fromagerie* in nearby Dayton to the Orchidaceae nursery, which ships plants nationwide—are suddenly thriving. There's even that ultimate validation of a burgeoning demographic: no fewer than five Starbucks dot the streets.

OPPOSITE: Dinner at the Whitehouse-Crawford restaurant. PREVIOUS SPREAD, FROM LEFT: Seven Hills Vineyard's harvest; a barn outside Walla Walla.

At the same time, gifted winemakers and resourceful businessmen are streaming in, seeking America's next great viticultural region or simply a fresh start, filling those once empty parking spots. Raised in Seattle, Nina Buty studied art history at Walla Walla's Whitman College, then left to travel the world. By chance, she married a local oenologist—Caleb Foster, who'd worked at the pioneering winery Woodward Canyon—and returned in 2001 to help him create Buty Winery, in a concrete hut beside the Walla Walla airport. Plans for a showcase facility with a sculpture garden are off in the future; for now, all resources go into the wines. Foster's oenology texts share shelf space with Buty's art books, and their crisp Chardonnays and dense Cabernet- and Merlot-based blends serve as both commercial products and Buty's artistic statements. "In a sense, making a wine is just like building a sculpture," she says.

As she steers into the parking lot of the Foundry, where works by Deborah Butterfield are displayed beside Chuck Ginnever's bronze castings and the works of local sculptors, Buty tells me she never thought she'd live in Walla Walla once she left

Whitman. "Creativity has always been here, but before now the ideas were only sustainable for a month or two," she says. "Restaurants would open with all kinds of ambition, but they couldn't stay in business for long. Now, with the influx of money, and people who have come to Walla Walla to enjoy the wine, we've reached a critical mass."

WALLA WALLA MAY NOT TURN INTO ANOTHER Napa, because the closest big city, Seattle, is a five-hour drive away over a mountain pass (whereas Napa is only an hour's drive from the Golden Gate Bridge). But it does seem poised to become America's second destination for wine tourism. Dayton's Weinhard Café, downtown's Backstage Bistro, and the Whitehouse-Crawford—which reinvented Washington dining east of the Cascades when it opened in 2000—have recast restaurant meals here from rudimentary pit stops to something you can plan a night around. What you ate, and the wine you drank with it, are now prime topics of conversation during coffee breaks at businesses around town. Of course, it doesn't hurt that many of those businesses are wineries.

The first Walla Walla wine I tried, back in the early nineties, was Rick Small's 1988 Woodward Canyon Cabernet Sauvignon. At the time, it struck me as the best American bottling I'd come across that wasn't from California. Then I uncovered one of Gary Figgins's Leonetti Merlots, a wine that had been just a rumor to me for years, and several impressive releases from L'Ecole No. 41, which is set in an old schoolhouse in nearby Lowden, Washington. I was a believer.

Small and Figgins, Army Reserve buddies, started Walla Walla's wine industry as a glorified home-economics project in the late seventies. They began on a modest scale, trucking in fruit from other parts of the state, not having any notion that Merlot and Cabernet would actually flourish amid the wheat and sweet onions. They made wine in Walla Walla only because they lived in Walla Walla. But L'Ecole's Martin Clubb, the son of a Texas oilman, has a business degree from MIT. He'd spent time in Boston, Philadelphia, and San Francisco. What, I couldn't help but wonder, had brought him here?

It turns out that his wife, Megan, has century-old Walla Walla roots that run deeper than the oldest vines. Megan's father, Baker Ferguson, was running Walla Walla's biggest bank when he started L'Ecole in 1983. He soon learned that you can't manage a winery as a hobby—not a successful one, anyway. So he dangled the possibility of an eventual position at the bank to lure his daughter home from San Francisco, where she had a high-powered finance job, and told her to bring along that husband of hers to handle L'Ecole.

Clubb took to the wine business, and soon L'Ecole was thriving. But the transition from San Francisco was a struggle for the Clubbs. Walla Walla seemed smaller than its 33,000 inhabitants, in part because nobody new ever moved in. "It was the kind of place," Clubb recalls, "where, if you dialed a wrong number, you knew the person who answered the phone."

The change happened so fast, locals like the Clubbs didn't see it coming. First, two wineries set up tasting rooms on Main Street. Then, the once glamorous Marcus Whitman Hotel, built by a civic consortium in 1927 as a local showpiece but converted to subsistence housing in the late seventies, was restored by a Walla Walla organization headed by cell phone millionaire Kyle Mussman. His group gutted the interior, creating a hotel and conference center. The guest rooms had handcrafted desks, DVD players, two-line phones, terry-cloth bathrobes, and a higher

WHAT YOU EAT, AND THE WINE YOU DRINK WITH IT, ARE PRIME TOPICS OF CONVERSATION DURING COFFEE BREAKS AROUND TOWN

level of luxury than the area had known. Until the first 75 deluxe rooms opened in February 2001, Walla Walla had had few visitors, only aspirations.

In retrospect, the Marcus Whitman Hotel was the tipping point. Today, the property isn't always full, or even close to it, and the service doesn't quite reach the level of the appointments. (By appearances, half the staff is still enrolled in high school, and breakfast—even on weekday mornings—means a visit to a nearby Denny's.) But its mere existence signifies that local money has faith in the city's future. Watching the stream of well-heeled hotel guests during one of the several formal tasting weekends held each year at area wineries, it's impossible for Walla Walla residents not to think of themselves as shareholders in a stock destined to rise.

All week, I've been holed up at the Inn at Abeja, a three-cottage and two-suite bed-and-breakfast in a restored farmstead a few miles east of downtown. My split-level suite has Wi-Fi, a CD player I haven't had time to use, and several hundred channels of DirecTV. The bookcases are stuffed with authors I actually want to read, from David Sedaris to F. Scott Fitzgerald, and the cabinets are stocked with Riedel stemware to show off the local wine. At breakfast on my first morning, I found fresh mango chunks awaiting me, and juice that had been inside the orange moments before. Lucinda Williams was singing on the sound system, and poached eggs and warm bread were headed my way. I could have stayed there all day.

OPPOSITE, FROM FAR LEFT: A bedroom at the Inn at Abeja; Nina Buty, an owner of Buty Winery, with Kahlou, at the top of Scenic Loop Road overlooking Walla Walla Valley.

In the B&B's Locust Suite, with its Craftsman-style cabinets and slate floors, I notice pencil marks scratched on the wooden walls. Dating back to the mid-1940's, they record the maintenance status of the farm vehicles. I see that a Pierce Arrow needed an oil change; I find myself hoping someone attended to it before the transmission balked. For a

THE ENERGY IN THE RESTAURANT'S DINING ROOM COULD POWER THE CITY FOR AN ENTIRE WEEK

moment, I visualize what it must have been like here on a September day when that long-departed Pierce still had a fresh coat of paint. The wheat farmers would have been busy stocking provisions against the coming cold; unlike winery owners, they had no $50-a-bottle cases of Merlot to ship to customers during bleak months.

ALMOST FROM THE DAY THE WHITEHOUSE-Crawford Restaurant opened in 2000, the L-shaped bar tucked into a corner of its dining room has served as an unofficial clubhouse for the town's wine-and-food community. It isn't just because a winery, Seven Hills, shares the same circa-1904 mill building, separated only by a wall of glass—and it certainly isn't the draconian corkage fee that the restaurant imposes on anyone who wants to drink his own wine with dinner, even if he made the wine himself. Jamie Guerin's menu is as urbane as any in eastern Washington (house-made tagliatelle with Oregon white truffle butter; wild mushroom croquettes with *piquillo* pepper sauce; a cassoulet of duck confit, pork belly, and garlic sausage), and the high-ceilinged space makes you feel sophisticated each time you step through its doors. The waitstaff moves briskly; the bartender has that big-city twinkle in his eye. The hardwood floors, exposed brick, and open kitchen place the restaurant's sensibility somewhere between San Francisco and Seattle, with just a bit of New York bustle thrown in.

On a Thursday night, I'm sipping wine there with K Vintners owner Charles Smith, who used to manage rock bands in Copenhagen. At 53, Smith has the hair of a heavy-metal guitarist and an irreverent manner that just about mandates self-

employment. "I didn't want my future to be decided by the talents of other people and the whims of the record business," he tells me. Instead, he returned to wine, his first love: he'd been a sommelier at the Ritz-Carlton, Rancho Mirage in his early twenties. If anything, his iconoclastic style has become more pronounced. He keeps a '49 Cadillac parked in the driveway of his winery, and has painted a huge block letter *K* on the front door. And yet his Syrahs may be the most graceful this side of Hermitage.

"Three people showed up at the tasting room the other day, and I wasn't in the mood for it," he reports. He tells me that he handed out glasses, then gave a droning, half-hour monologue about wine making while his visitors waited for something to drink. Finally, Smith led them to the barrel room and flicked a switch that filled the room with the booming chords of Led Zeppelin, and the tasting was on. An hour later, the visitors staggered into the light, dazed but gratified. I was sipping Smith's Pepperbridge Vineyard Syrah, so I knew why. His Syrahs—the left-of-center grape variety that provides the bulk of his tiny output—have the heft of heavy metal, but on the palate they're all Billie Holiday.

As Smith's story ends, I notice Christophe Baron, the Champagne-born proprietor of Cayuse Vineyards, striding toward our table with a wine bottle in each hand. To our left is another winemaker we all know, and at a table beyond is a chef I met earlier in the week. My food—braised halibut with sweet peppers, then steak with gnocchi and a smoky, leather-scented *chimichurri* sauce—is infused with the ambition of a chef who wants to make a difference, and the energy in the room could power the city for an entire week. I leave at midnight, intoxicated by a sense of limitless possibilities—and an awful lot of the local wine.

THE NEXT MORNING I WALK OFF THE MEAL with a stroll along Main Street, from one end of downtown to another. I pass a street-corner sculpture I haven't seen before, and just beyond it an Internet café selling gourmet jams and jellies. The *New York Times* is on sale at Starbucks, and two cars with California plates are parked outside the Waterbrook Winery tasting room. Most of all, I can't help but notice, there's not a single tumbleweed in sight.

OPPOSITE: Main Street, in downtown Walla Walla.

GETTING THERE

There are two daily flights to Walla Walla from Seattle, but the closest airport with direct flights from Portland, Oregon, and Denver is in Pasco, an hour away. Summers in southeastern Washington are dry, with daylight lasting late into the evening—one reason the grapes tend to ripen so well. The shoulder season (spring and fall) lingers, giving way to more extreme weather only after weeks of breezy sunshine.

WHERE TO STAY

Green Gables Inn Six-room B&B with historic touches that include Art Nouveau armoires and claw-foot tubs, in a 1909 house on the Whitman College campus. *922 Bonsella St.; 509/525-5501; greengablesinn.com; doubles from $.*

Inn at Abeja Circa-1900 property where each of the three cottages and two suites are different, from floor plan to interiors. *2014 Mill Creek Rd.; 509/522-1234; abeja.net; suites from $, including breakfast; closed mid-December through late February.*

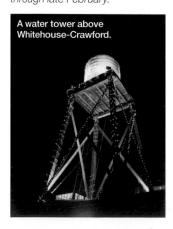

A water tower above Whitehouse-Crawford.

Marcus Whitman Hotel Urbane 1928 property with ornate accents and a modern wing, near the restaurants and tasting rooms of Main Street. *6 W. Rose St.; 866/826-9422 or 509/525-2200; marcuswhitmanhotel.com; doubles from $.*

WHERE TO EAT

Backstage Bistro Eclectic New American bistro in a gallery setting. *230 E. Main St.; 509/526-0690; dinner for two XX.*

Weinhard Café Storefront steak house with frilly accents, located across the street from a Victorian hotel in rural Dayton, Washington (which is a short drive from Walla Walla). *258 E. Main St., Dayton; 509/382-1681; dinner for two XX.*

Whitehouse-Crawford Ambitious cooking, an extensive list of Washington State wines, and the most sophisticated scene in town. *55 W. Cherry St.; 509/525-2222; dinner for two XXX.*

WINERIES

Walla Walla's producers are far more informal than those in Napa. This means that face-to-face encounters with winemakers are eminently possible, but it also means you should call ahead to make sure someone will be there when you arrive.

Buty Winery Known for beefy reds and a full-throttle Chardonnay, in a glorified Quonset hut by the airport. *535 E. Cessna Ave.; 509/527-0901; butywinery.com.*

Cayuse Vineyards Washington's most accomplished Syrah, along with sophisticated blends that belie their cartoonish labels. *17 E. Main St.; 509/526-0686; cayusevineyards.com.*

Dunham Cellars The Syrahs and Cabernets here are world-class. *150 E. Boeing Ave.; 509/529-4685; dunhamcellars.com.*

K Vintners Offbeat producer Charles Smith makes complex

A vintage handcrafted bar at the Inn at Abeja.

Rhône-style Syrahs. *820 Mill Creek Rd.; 509/526-5230; kvintners.com.*

L'Ecole No. 41 Taste consistently good wines made in a restored schoolhouse on the road to Pasco. *Dry Creek Rd. and Hwy. 12, Lowden; 509/525-0940; lecole.com.*

Seven Hills Winery Drink sturdy Cabernets, Merlots, and blends at a tasting room adjoining the Whitehouse-Crawford dining room. *212 N. Third Ave.; 877/777-7870; sevenhillswinery.com.*

Woodward Canyon Winery A Walla Walla original that still produces some of the more reasonably priced vintages, including elegant and ageworthy Cabernets and Merlots. *11920 W. Hwy. 12, Lowden; 509/525-4129; woodwardcanyon.com.*

Wine barrels at L'Ecole No. 41.

A sculpture by artist Ed Humpherys at the Walla Walla Foundry. RIGHT: Owners Mark and Joan Baleman, of Orchidaceae.

Top Four Non-Wine Activities

Blue Mountain Lavender Farm
The Grimaud family emigrated here from France in 1997, never imagining that guests would soon wander through their aromatic fields of 15 types of lavender (and, for a small fee, pluck their own). *345 Short Rd., Lowden; 509/529-3276; bluemountain lavender.com.*

Monteillet Fromagerie Sample Walla Walla wines paired with freshly made goat cheese (the herbed chèvre is blended with organic basil, chives, cilantro, and parsley—all grown here). *109 Ward Rd., Dayton; 509/382-1917; monteilletcheese.com.*

Orchidaceae Set between rolling fields, greenhouses hold oncidium, phalaenopsis, and cattleya orchids, as well as dozens of other plant varieties. *2022 Wallula Ave.; 509/525-9566; orchidaceae.com.*

Walla Walla Foundry A workshop for artists and a sculpture garden of pieces produced on site (including some by Deborah Butterfield and Jim Dine). *405 Woodland Ave.; 509/522-2114; walla wallafoundry.com.*

Crystals at CityCenter, in Las Vegas.

The Glass Pavilion, in Toledo, Ohio.

At work on the Sol LeWitt retrospective at MASS MoCA, in the Berkshires.

Sculptures by John Chamberlain in Marfa, Texas.

ARTS + CULTURE

Photographed by David Cicconi

MASS TRANSIT

A WHIRLWIND TOUR OF THE ART-RICH BERKSHIRES LEADS TO AN AMBITIOUS
RETROSPECTIVE BY CONCEPTUAL MASTER SOL LEWITT. BY GABRIELLA DE FERRARI

SINCE I FIRST TRAVELED TO THE BERKSHIRES TO VISIT THE CLARK ART INSTITUTE,

Part of artist Sol LeWitt's instructions for his MASS MoCA retrospective, below. OPPOSITE, FROM TOP: The North Fairchild Gallery at Amherst College's Mead Art Museum; the 17th-century Rotherwas Court room at the Mead. Previous spread: LeWitt's wall drawings at MASS MoCA.

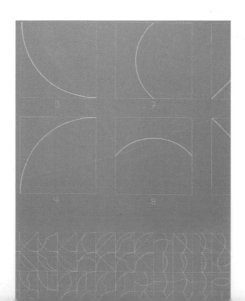

in Williamstown, Massachusetts, I've returned to explore the region more times than I can remember. But this trip, with my friend Carol LeWitt, would be a special pilgrimage: a four-day exploration of the Berkshires' most revered museums that would culminate in a visit to MASS MoCA, home to a wall-drawing retrospective honoring her late husband, Sol LeWitt. The conceptual artist died in April 2007 at the age of 78 while working on the exhibition, which opened in November 2008.

Thanks in part to the largesse of their alumni, the area's colleges (Smith, Amherst, University of Massachusetts Amherst, Williams, and Mount Holyoke) possess museums that have helped turn the Berkshires into a thriving arts destination. No other pastoral region in the United States can lay claim to so many ambitious and architecturally inspiring art institutions, all within two hours' drive of one another.

DAY 1: NEW YORK TO NORTHAMPTON

After 3½ hours on the road, we arrive at the town of Northampton, site of our first stop: the Smith College Museum of Art. A large majority of the artworks here are gifts of alumnae—many of whom started donating their prized possessions in the early 1900's. A $35 million renovation transformed the simple concrete structure into a soaring steel-and-red-brick Modernist creation with enormous light-filled galleries. The art collection spans more than 4,500 years. We see works by 19th- and 20th-century masters such as Gustave Courbet, Ernst Ludwig Kirchner, Jean Arp, and Pablo Picasso. I find the most riveting piece to be an oil painting called *Old Man Writing by Candlelight,* by the 17th-century Dutch artist Hendrick Terbrugghen, whose work is rarely seen in the United States. Caravaggio strongly influenced Terbrugghen, and like the late-Renaissance painter, he contrasts light and dark dramatically: a burning candle illuminates the old man's face to reveal a map of wrinkles so intricate that he appears to come alive on the canvas.

There's a Sol LeWitt drawing to see here before we move on to the exhibition at MASS MoCA. The work, titled *Wall Drawing #139 (Grid and arcs from the midpoints of four sides)* (1972), is one of the artist's signature geometric pencil drawings,

covering an entire 21-by-11-foot gallery wall. The wall-drawing series was revolutionary because it proposed the idea that an artist's concept was more important than its actual execution. "To see this work realized is remarkable, since I'd only read Sol's instructions on how to re-create it," Carol says. LeWitt would initially come up with the idea, then write instructions that would allow any trained draftsman to bring his vision to life.

Northampton is no longer the strict New England community it was during the early 20th century, when Calvin Coolidge was mayor here. It is college-town central, located only two hours west of Boston. The tidy streets are lined with health-food delis, independent bookstores, and buzzing cafés, all packed with loitering students. I try in vain to find a diet Coke in shops that sell only natural and organic drinks; and at the bookstore where Carol and I buy works by Orhan Pamuk and Andrea Camilleri, the eco-conscious salesclerk assumes we'd rather take our purchases home without a bag.

We check in to our home base for the next two days, the Hotel Northampton, a 1927 Colonial Revival building in the center of town, before heading to the Tibetan restaurant Lhasa Café. I expect the typically bland food you usually find in a college town, but the yak is spicy and tender. Paired with a glass of robust Cabernet, it's the perfect end to the day.

DAY 2: NORTHAMPTON TO AMHERST

Eight miles northeast and across the Connecticut River, our next stop is the Fine Arts Center at the University of Massachusetts Amherst. The concrete box, designed by architects Kevin Roche and John Dinkeloo in 1975, comes across as anything but welcoming, though it houses a concert hall and a contemporary art gallery that has mounted ambitious temporary exhibitions of such notable artists as Tom Friedman and Gabriel Orozco, garnering international recognition.

A five-minute drive south is the Mead Art Museum at Amherst College. The institution is known as a compact bastion of American treasures—Robert Henri's *Salome* (1909) is housed here—so we're happily surprised by the selection of Russian art. Most are the gifts of one collector, Thomas P. Whitney, class of 1937, who moved to Moscow, married a Russian pianist, and cultivated one of the most discerning collections of modern Russian masterpieces in the United States. We were particularly moved by the 20th-century avant-garde paintings by Liubov Popova and Natalia Goncharova. Sculptor Alexander Archipenko's *Torso in Space* (1936), a sensuous bronze replica of a nude female figure, appears to float in air despite its decidedly earthbound pedestal. These treasures are too personal in nature to have been assembled by a museum curator, whose objective is often to tell the history of art. Instead, they reveal the passion and taste of one avid collector.

DAY 3: AMHERST TO WILLIAMSTOWN

We set out early for the 1½-hour drive to the Sterling and Francine Clark Art Institute, eager to see the Stone Hill Center, designed by the Japanese architect Tadao Ando. Seeing the Pritzker Prize winner's Modern Art Museum, in Fort Worth, Texas, was a memorable experience for Carol and me, so we're expecting Stone Hill, his third U.S. project, to be equally impressive. It is: as we round the entranceway into the museum, Ando's building rises ever so subtly from the wooded hillside, as if part of the landscape; its sharp lines, broad flat planes, and geometric precision blend with the mountains that loom in the background.

We've asked the Clark's director, Michael Conforti, to walk us through the center, 12,000 square feet of conservation workspace and two glass-walled galleries. Ando's design pulls the outdoors in as a companion to the exhibitions.

A walk down the hill brings us to the original museum, a glowing white-marble temple that

momentarily takes you out of rural Williamstown and puts you in Athens. Architect Daniel Perry designed the Neoclassical building, which was completed in 1955. Its scholarly collection of masterpieces set a new standard for museums in the area. To me, the Clark is for reconnecting with an old friend—the museum owns one of only five Piero della Francescas in the United States:

MORE THAN 50 DRAFTERS WERE HIRED BY MASS MOCA TO PUT THE NEARLY ONE-ACRE RETROSPECTIVE TOGETHER

Virgin and Child Enthroned with Four Angels (circa 1460–70). Surely the most explicit depiction of the wonderment of motherhood I've ever seen, it draws me back here again and again.

Especially after communing with Ando, Charles Moore's 1980's postmodern overhaul of the Williams College Museum of Art looks dated and fussy to me now—but it did put this small liberal arts college on the global art map. At the entrance stands *Eyes* (2001), massive gray marble slabs with round, watchful eyes perched on top, by phenomenal Paris-born sculptor Louise Bourgeois. Carol and I both know where we're going: straight to Edward Hopper's *Morning in a City* (1944), one of our favorites here. A nude female peers out of an open bedroom window, the front of her bathed in sunlight, her back cast in shadows, with somber shades of greens and blues in the background. As in most of his oil paintings, Hopper's enigmatic way with light keeps a viewer rapt and respectful before the most ordinary of scenes. It is a standout in a collection known for its contemporary art.

DAY 4: WILLIAMSTOWN TO NORTH ADAMS

Just 10 minutes southeast down Route 2 leads us to MASS MoCA, where we've decided to try another hotel. The retro-chic Porches, 47 rooms in a row of restored Victorian-era buildings that once housed the town's mill workers, is just across the street. The hotel could be in any tony New England community, but down the road there are empty warehouses with shattered windows, shuttered shops, and almost no

one in sight—signs of the economic depression from which the once-industrial area is slowly recovering. MASS MoCA has been a catalyst for change in this community. The museum is a village in miniature spread over 13 acres, with 25 buildings dedicated to art, music, dance, film, and theater.

A series of gigantic red-brick warehouses (this was a textile mill in the early 20th century) makes up this one-of-a-kind cultural center, which in less than a decade has become New England's most innovative art space. I'm in awe of its sheer size as we traverse miles of raw gallery space flooded with light, one room the size of a football field. Carol mentions that what Sol had thought was missing in the United States was a museum dedicated to installations. MASS MoCA certainly fills this vacuum; no other institution can showcase exhibits of such immense proportions. This is the largest center for contemporary visual and performing arts in the country.

When the exhibition was being arranged by Jock Reynolds, director of the Yale University Art Gallery, and Joseph C. Thompson, director of MASS MoCA, Carol and Sol visited the 27,000-square-foot former mill building where it would be housed. "I watched him climb up and down ladders to develop his plan for the installation, studying the light, the placements of the drawings," she says. Now she was seeing his vision become reality. Everything has been built to LeWitt's specifications: he placed all the interior walls and preserved all the windows to flood the space with natural light. More than 50 drafters were hired by the museum to put this nearly one-acre retrospective together.

MASS MOCA WILL KEEP THE RETROSPECTIVE on view here until at least 2033. At first, it might seem incongruous that one of the most important contemporary masters in the world would be enshrined in a corner of the Berkshire Hills. But given the scale and magnitude of the exhibition— and the growing artistic movement in this part of New England—it actually is a most fitting memorial. For the foreseeable future, this remote area will become a site for all who love the work of Sol LeWitt, and art itself.

WHEN TO GO
Spring through fall, when festivals abound and small cultural sites are open, is a great time for art tours in the Berkshires. Autumn foliage peaks in early to mid-October. Book well in advance for the month of May, as visitors descend on the region for graduation ceremonies.

WHERE TO STAY
Deerfield Inn Country inn from the 19th century, with English parlors and an on-site tavern. *81 Main St., Deerfield; 800/926-3865 or 413/774-5587; deerfieldinn.com; doubles from $.*
Harbour House Inn Six bright, cheerful rooms with floral prints, pedestal sinks, and claw-foot tubs, in an 18th-century Georgian Colonial mansion. *725 N. State Rd., Cheshire; 413/743-8959; harbourhouseinn.com; doubles from $.*
Hotel Northampton Located three blocks from Smith College, with a 200-year-old tavern that was moved from New Hampshire and meticulously reassembled. *36 King St., Northampton; 800/547-3529 or 413/584-3100; hotelnorthampton.com; doubles from $.*
Old Inn on the Green Stagecoach relay turned 11-room lodge with authentic period furniture. *134 Hartsville New Marlborough Rd., Rte. 57, Village Green, New Marlborough; 413/229-7924;*

oldinn.com; doubles from $.
Porches Inn Crisp, sweetly retro rooms in a row of renovated Victorian houses. *231 River St., North Adams; 413/664-0400; porches.com; doubles from $.*
Topia Inn Eco-friendly bed-and-breakfast run by two artists; several of the rooms have chromatherapy spa tubs. *10 Pleasant St., Adams; 413/743-9605; topiainn.com; doubles from $.*

WHERE TO EAT
Chez Nous Classic French bistro with New England touches. *150 Main St., Lee; 413/243-6397; dinner for two XXX.*
Eastside Grill Upscale seasonal American fare. *19 Strong Ave., Northampton; 413/586-3347; dinner for two XX.*

Amenities at the Porches Inn.

Gramercy Bistro at MASS MoCA Popular establishment that relocated to the museum in early 2010. *87 Marshall St., North Adams; 413/663-5300; lunch for two XX.*
Judie's Restaurant Local institution famous for its popovers, like the "turkey pop pie" (stuffed with sliced turkey simmered in a mushroom-Madeira sauce). *51 N. Pleasant St., Amherst; 413/253-3491; dinner for two XX.*
Lhasa Café Authentic Tibetan cuisine in the heart of downtown. *159 Main St., Northampton; 413/586-5427; dinner for two XX.*
Tabellas Farm-to-table dishes, like a Berkshire pork loin served with red-pepper relish and herbed potato pancake. *28 Amity St., Amherst; 413/253-0220; dinner for two XXX.*

WHERE TO SHOP
Broadside Bookshop Indie literary establishment that hosts regular readings. *247 Main St., Northampton; 413/586-4235.*
Cupboards & Roses Good source for Scandinavian antiques, including folk art, 19th-century hope chests, and hand-painted armoires. *296 S. Main St., Sheffield; 413/229-3070.*
Guild Art Supply A seemingly bottomless inventory of art supplies, plus a frame shop and letterpress studio. *102 Main St., Northampton; 800/479-6343 or 413/586-6343.*

Montague Book Mill In a former gristmill, cozy reading nooks and a stock of more than a thousand titles. *440 Greenfield Rd., Montague; 413/367-9206.*

Pine Cone Hill Sophisticated home textiles from designer Annie Selke. *55 Pittsfield Rd., Lenox; 413/637-1996.*

Thornes Marketplace More than 20 clothing, jewelry, and crafts stores in a century-old building with pressed-tin ceilings. *150 Main St., Northampton; 413/584-5582.*

WHAT TO SEE + DO

Ashuwillticook Rail Trail Eleven-mile corridor converted to a hiking and biking trail, winding through the Hoosic River Valley wetlands from Lanesboro to Adams. *mass.gov/dcr/parks/western/asrt.htm.*

Hancock Shaker Village Educational center and living museum that hosts seminars, Shaker suppers, and an annual country fair. *184 W. Housatonic St., Pittsfield; 800/817-1137; hancockshakervillage.org.*

Hilltop Orchards Hundred-year-old farm that grows 27 varieties of apples; most are available for picking. *Rte. 295/508 Canaan Rd., Richmond; 800/833-6274; hilltoporchards.com.*

Historic Deerfield New England village lined with 18th-century clapboard houses; nine are open to the public for self-guided or group tours. *413/774-5581; historic-deerfield.org.*

The Mount Novelist Edith Wharton's artfully landscaped estate hosts garden tours from May to October. *2 Plunkett St., Lenox; 413/551-5100; edithwharton.org.*

New England Falconry Learn how to handle and free-fly hawks during 45-minute to three-hour sessions. *Hadley; 413/259-1466; newenglandfalconry.com.*

MUSEUMS

Fine Arts Center, University of Massachusetts Amherst Contemporary art gallery and concert hall. *151 Presidents Dr., Amherst; 800/999-8627; fineartscenter.com.*

MASS MoCA Spread out over 13 acres, a former textile mill turned groundbreaking gallery space and arts center. *1040 MASS MoCA Way, North Adams; 413/662-2111; massmoca.org.*

Mead Art Museum Home to a permanent collection of more than 16,000 works, including modern Russian masterpieces. *41 Quadrangle Rd., Amherst; 413/542-2335; amherst.edu/mead.*

Mount Holyoke College Art Museum One of the first college art museums in the country. *Lower Lake Rd., South Hadley; 413/538-2245; mtholyoke.edu/artmuseum.*

Smith College Museum of Art Four floors of galleries just up the hill from downtown Northampton. *Elm St. at Bedford Terrace, Northampton; 413/585-2760; smith.edu/museum.*

Sterling and Francine Clark Art Institute Permanent collection best known for French impressionist and Italian Renaissance works.

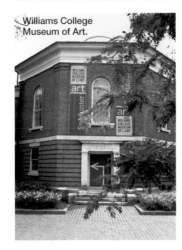

Williams College Museum of Art.

225 South St., Williamstown; 413/458-2303; clarkart.edu.

Stone Hill Center Tadao Ando–designed structure housing two new galleries of the Sterling and Francine Clark Art Institute. *225 South St., Williamstown; 413/458-2303; clarkart.edu.*

Williams College Museum of Art Works include a top-notch collection of American art from the late 18th century to the present. *15 Lawrence Hall Dr., Williamstown; 413/597 2429; wcma.org.*

FESTIVALS

Brimfield Antiques Show Three times yearly, this outdoor *brocante*—6,000 stalls stretched across 23 fields—hits the little town of Brimfield. Serious collectors start at the crack of dawn to get first dibs on vintage finds. *Exits 8 and 9 off the Massachusetts Turnpike (I-90); brimfieldshow.com; May, July, and September.*

Jacob's Pillow Dance Festival Founded in 1932, this annual celebration is the longest-running dance festival in the nation, attracting more than 50 ballet, jazz, modern, and experimental dance troupes, including such boldface names as Alvin Ailey and Merce Cunningham. *358 George Carter Rd., Becket; 413/243-0745; jacobspillow.org; mid-June through August.*

Tanglewood Hands down the Berkshires' most famous festival, drawing more than 250,000 visitors—and scores of world-class musicians—annually. *297 West St., Lenox; 888/266-1200; tanglewood.org; late June to early September.*

Williamstown Theatre Festival Grand showcase of the region's top productions and summer stock theater at its best (it even won a Tony Award in 2002). *Located on the Williams College campus; 413/597-3399; wtfestival.org; June to August.*

Fun in the Berkshires

MASS MoCA director Joseph C. Thompson shares five non-art-related favorites.

AERIAL VIEWS "Flying over the Berkshires is thrilling. And Harriman-and-West Airport, in North Adams, at the base of Mount Greylock, is one of the most scenic airports in the United States."

BREWSKIES AND WINGS "At **Old Forge Restaurant** *(125 N. Main St., Lanesboro; 413/442-6797; dinner for two* **XX***),* the beer—more than a hundred different varieties—and chicken wings are world-class."

CROSS-COUNTRY SKIING "There's a great trail at **Field Farm** *(thetrustees.org/field-farm),* the estate of modern art collectors Lawrence and Eleanor Bloedel."

CYCLING "Thanks to the wide shoulders on Route Seven from Williamstown to New Ashford, biking here is terrific. Once the Ashuwillticook Rail Trail loops around the base of Mount Greylock, wending through orchards and meadows, it will be an attraction of Tanglewood-size proportions."

MUSICAL PREVIEWS "I love the indie music at MASS MoCA's Alt Cab series—you can hear future stars sing at our own Club B-10 six months before they make it big."

KEY TO THE DINING PRICE ICONS   **X** UNDER $25   **XX** $25–$74   **XXX** $75–$149   **XXXX** $150–$299   **XXXXX** $300 AND UP

Photographed by Kevin J. Miyazaki

DESIGN IN THE HEARTLAND

WANT A FIRSTHAND LOOK AT SOME OF THE COUNTRY'S MOST INSPIRING BUILDINGS? GO ON A ROAD TRIP THROUGH THE MIDWEST. BY OLIVER STRAND

IT MAY COME AS A SURPRISE, ESPECIALLY TO Midwesterners, but right now the most exciting architecture in America can be found in the Midwest. It all started in 2001, when the gleaming Santiago Calatrava addition to the Milwaukee Art Museum opened: suddenly, art lovers from around the world were going out of their way to visit a place once tagged as the buckle of the Rust Belt. Call it the ongoing Bilbao Effect. Frank Gehry's sinuous Guggenheim Museum transformed Spain's forgotten industrial city into a cultural mecca; Calatrava's work has made Milwaukee an architectural destination.

With 10 major projects completed in the past decade, including Calatrava's, now is the ideal time for a Midwestern architecture road trip. So I charted a loop that would take me from Ohio north to Illinois, Wisconsin, and Minnesota, then down through Iowa. This route also put me in the heart of Dairyland, and the trip turned out to be as much about ice cream as architecture. It's a natural combination here. The Midwest is one of the few places in the world where you can see a frenetic Rem Koolhaas building one day, then eat the biggest frozen-custard sundae of your life the next.

DAY 1: CINCINNATI

The labyrinthine complex of Morphosis-designed buildings at the University of Cincinnati is a monster: 350,000 square feet of classrooms, student dining, and a gym topped by a massive dorm—a V-shaped, cantilevered superblock with a chunk missing in the middle. It's an electrifying and disorienting jumble, and not a little sinister. Visitors can buy day passes to the gym, and from the enormous pool to the elliptical skylight, it's more beautiful than any spa I've seen. I was transfixed by the indoor track suspended above the basketball courts, especially the way it slices through the air ducts.

When I was a teenager in Los Angeles, it was a treat to eat at the Angeli Caffe, a restaurant designed by Morphosis that held no more than 20 people; now, here were hundreds of students in sweatpants and sandals lined up for lunch at Center Court, a dining hall decorated with 10-foot-high images of blades of grass. It looks like the coolest restaurant in some Scandinavian city, though the kids I saw seemed too wrapped up in their Wi-Fi to notice.

Next, I checked out architect Zaha Hadid's Contemporary Arts Center, a resolutely urban building nested into a corner lot in the middle of Cincinnati's downtown. The jutting concrete-and-glass structure is bursting with energy, like a kit of parts that could be pulled into pieces and reassembled. Inside, it's just as kinetic: the columns are trapezoids, the doors are parallelograms, and the stairways cross with such an unusual rhythm that you don't even realize they hide the third floor.

OPPOSITE: Architect Santiago Calatrava's addition to the Milwaukee Art Museum.

TOP, FROM LEFT:
The Toledo Art
Museum's Glass
Pavilion; a hallway
at the Milwaukee
Art Museum; the
Des Moines Public
Library's façade.
BELOW: Inside
the Des Moines
Public Library.

the glass-making rooms, and the frigid Lake Erie air outside differ wildly, and wherever the walls are made out of glass, they couldn't hide ducts or cables, so the machinery that regulates temperature is snaked to one of two opaque rooms, then carried along the ceiling. Even the air-conditioning units are located across the street so that they won't interrupt the roofline.

DAY 3: TOLEDO TO CHICAGO, 252 MILES

Mies van der Rohe taught at the Illinois Institute of Technology and designed many of its buildings, so for architects the campus is already hallowed ground. His use of crisp boxes made with brick, glass, and steel I-beams is a triumph of mid-20th-century design. Which is why IIT's awarding of the student center project to the Office for Metropolitan Architecture, headed by iconoclast Rem Koolhaas, was a real head-scratcher.

The result—completed in 2003—is the closest thing to punk a building can be. Its official name is the McCormick Tribune Campus Center, but one nickname for it is the BUT (Building Under a Tube), because it looks as if it's been scrunched under the enormous stainless-steel tube encompassing the elevated train track. The ceiling drywall has been left unprimed and unpainted, the bathroom walls are translucent, and several surfaces that look like wood veneer are, in fact, covered with wallpaper. After the BUT, Frank Gehry's Jay Pritzker Pavilion, in Millennium Park, feels thoughtful and earnest.

DAY 2: CINCINNATI TO TOLEDO, 210 MILES

It's a straight shot from Cincinnati to Toledo, Ohio, on I-75, with only two distractions to break up the drive: at Monroe, just north of Cincinnati, a five-story-high bust of Jesus towers over the interstate; in Findlay, 40 minutes south of Toledo, it's a short hop to Dietsch Brothers Inc., where they make their ice cream right in the back. I spent summers in Findlay with my grandparents, and when I tried the orange sherbet on this trip, it tasted like 1981.

The empty lots and boarded-up buildings in Toledo's downtown don't make for an inviting landscape, so the Toledo Museum of Art's decision to hire SANAA, a critically admired Japanese firm, seems even more remarkable. The SANAA-designed Glass Pavilion is simple enough—a one-story glass box encasing a series of glass rooms—but what seems like a basic form is a surprisingly sophisticated building. With it, SANAA is doing nothing less than taking on the Glass House, Philip Johnson's masterpiece.

Glass is one of Toledo's major industries, and the pavilion features both exhibition halls and "hot shops," or glass-making rooms. When you stand in a gallery, you can look through glass walls to watch artists heating glass in a 2,000-degree furnace, then through the rest of the transparent building to the park outside—all in one uninterrupted view.

Such a simple idea is actually quite complicated to execute. The mechanics should appeal to architecture geeks: the temperatures of the gallery,

Architect Steven Holl's School of Art and Art History, at the University of Iowa, below.

It's easy to be cynical about a Gehry building now that he's a brand name, but the Jay Pritzker Pavilion has a marvelous form and has made what was once a useless chunk of land into a focal point for the city. The metal ribs soaring over the lawn are overkill for holding up lights and speakers, but they do turn the park into an outdoor room, a patio for all of Chicago.

DAY 4: CHICAGO TO MILWAUKEE, 88 MILES

The drive north from Chicago is thick with fast-moving traffic, and before you know it you're passing Racine, Wisconsin, home to Frank Lloyd Wright's finest project, the Johnson Wax Building. Shortly after that, you hit the I-43/I-894 bypass, and it's a three-minute detour to Kopp's (right off the 76th Street exit) for the Midwest's finest frozen custard. I first had a burger, but that was just to cushion the blow of the Peanut Butter Log: chocolate sauce piled high with frozen custard, then topped with nutty sauce and more chocolate.

Framed by Lake Michigan, Santiago Calatrava's Quadracci Pavilion at the Milwaukee Art Museum is unlike anything for hundreds of miles around, a form that evokes the shapes of ships (both sea and space); Wright's Marin County Civic Center; and the bones of a bird, bleached by the sun. Which is why it's a bit of a surprise to realize it's nothing more than the entrance hall for the museum, a 1950's Eero Saarinen bunker. Still, it has the optimism of a World's Fair building, a celebration of engineering and structure. You've never seen poured concrete used to such an ethereal effect.

DAY 5: MILWAUKEE TO MINNEAPOLIS, 337 MILES

The Herzog & de Meuron addition to the Walker Art Center, completed in 2005, looks like a monumental wad of crumpled tinfoil. This is a compliment: the perforated metal holds and deflects the light in unusual ways, making what is essentially a featureless box seem like a dynamic shape. The addition has only a handful of galleries: much of it is taken up by a performing arts theater. The adjacent building, which was once home to the Guthrie Theater, one of America's most important regional companies, was torn down and is now part of the Walker's parklike campus.

As for the Guthrie itself, in June 2006 it moved into a muscular Jean Nouvel building on a prominent

spot on the banks of the Mississippi River. Because the river is best seen from above, Nouvel put the lobby and main theaters on the fourth floor; through a plate-glass window in the lobby, you can watch workers wheel sets from the scene shop across an enclosed bridge.

DAY 6: MINNEAPOLIS TO DES MOINES, 258 MILES

The horizon of central Iowa is so featureless, you can spot downtown Des Moines from 10 miles away. In the middle of that staid but pleasant town is David Chipperfield's quietly radical Des Moines Public Library, a low-slung building clad in a perforated copper skin sandwiched between layers of glass. The footprint looks like a T cut out of construction paper, or maybe a stylized airplane, and that silhouette has become a symbol for the library. Despite its unusual shape and color, it's really a modest building (and much more original than his Figge Art Museum, across the state in Davenport, Iowa), just two stories of books and computers. Some of the flooring in the children's library is made out of glass, so you can see how the plumbing and Ethernet cables wind underfoot.

Before leaving town I paid a visit to the Des Moines Art Center, a quick drive along Grand to 45th Street. It's an elegant 1948 Eliel Saarinen museum with a fascinating I. M. Pei addition from the late 1960's. A Richard Meier wing was added in 1985; stand in the courtyard and you'll take in half a century of American architecture.

DAY 7: DES MOINES TO IOWA CITY, 114 MILES

After taking a peek at Louis Sullivan's 1914 Merchants National Bank, in Grinnell, and circuiting the campus of the University of Iowa, I found Steven Holl's School of Art and Art History, a hulk of a building sheathed in rusted Cor-Ten steel panels and cantilevered over the pond of an abandoned limestone quarry. Sadly, the building was damaged by flooding in 2008 and is currently closed for renovation, scheduled to reopen in spring 2011. Holl was also enlisted to design a replacement for another university building that was completely wrecked by the flood; the projected date for completion is 2014.

Across the Iowa River was my last stop: Whitey's Ice Cream, famous for its "Boston" (a shake with a sundae perched on top). It's rare to find ice cream this good—or architecture this edgy.

OPPOSITE: *Vitrana,* a 1970 glass mural by Dominick Labino, at Toledo's Glass Pavilion.

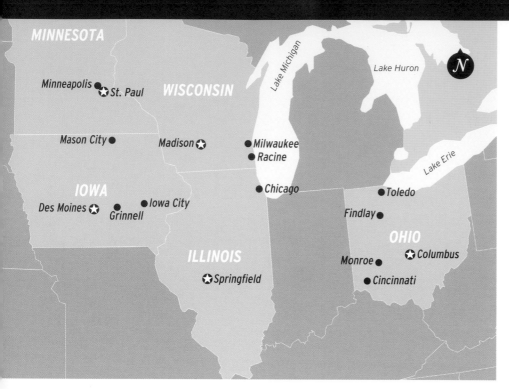

MINNESOTA

Minneapolis ● ✪ St. Paul

WISCONSIN

Lake Michigan

Lake Huron

N

Mason City ●   Madison ✪   ● Milwaukee
● Racine

IOWA   ● Chicago

Des Moines ✪   ● Iowa City
● Grinnell

Lake Erie

● Toledo

Findlay ●

OHIO

ILLINOIS

✪ Springfield   Monroe ●   ✪ Columbus
● Cincinnati

WHERE TO STAY

ILLINOIS
The Wit Buzzy downtown hotel with a lively rooftop bar. *201 N. State St., Chicago; 866/318-1514 or 312/467-0200; thewithotel.com; doubles from $.*

IOWA
Hotel Vetro Sophisticated, minimalist studio suites at affordable rates. *201 S. Linn St., Iowa City; 800/592-0355 or* 319/337-4961; hotelvetro.com; suites from $.

Suites of 800 Locust The lodging of choice for presidential candidates during caucuses. *800 Locust St., Des Moines; 800/320-2580 or 515/288-5800; 800locust.com; suites from $.*

MINNESOTA
Depot Renaissance Stately rooms in a former train station. *225 S. Third Ave., Minneapolis; 612/375-1700; thedepot minneapolis.com; doubles from $.*

OHIO
Hilton Cincinnati Netherland Plaza 1930's Art Deco landmark in the heart of the city. *35 W. Fifth St., Cincinnati; 800/445-8667 or 513/421-9100; cincinnatihilton.com; doubles from $.*

Mansion View Inn Five-room Victorian B&B just steps from the Toledo Museum of Art. *2035 Collingwood Blvd., Toledo; 419/244-5676; mansionview toledo.com; doubles from $.*

Inside the Wit hotel, in Chicago.

WISCONSIN
The Pfister Bastion of old-world civility since 1893, with 307 guest rooms and suites a few blocks from Lake Michigan. *424 E. Wisconsin Ave., Milwaukee; 800/558-8222 or 414/273-8222; thepfisterhotel.com; doubles from $.*

WHERE TO EAT

ILLINOIS
Chicago Firehouse Yellow-brick-and-limestone fire station from 1905, now the backdrop for classic American cuisine. *1401 S. Michigan Ave., Chicago; 312/786-1401; dinner for two ✖✖✖.*

IOWA
Basil Prosperi's Lucca Rooted in Tuscan tradition, with an excellent wine list. *420 E. Locust St., Des Moines; 515/243-1115; dinner for two ✖✖.*

Flarah's Popular lunch spot with a cheerful design sensibility. *2815 Beaver Ave., Des Moines; 515/277-1935; lunch for two ✖.*

MINNESOTA
Cosmos Sleek, cosmopolitan interior; the Swedish chef is known for bold flavor combinations, as in a scallop ceviche with chorizo mousse and galangal root. *601 First Ave. N., Minneapolis; 612/312-1168; dinner for two ✖✖✖.*

OHIO
JeanRo Eclectic bistro serving French and American staples. *413 Vine St., Cincinnati; 513/621-1465; dinner for two ✖✖✖.*

Ollie's Trolley Take-out grub served out of a vintage trolley car; famous for its Ollie burger and rib tips. *1607 Central Ave., Cincinnati; 513/381-6100; lunch for two ✖.*

Tony Packo's Café Kitschy favorite serving up Hungarian hot dogs since the Great Depression. *1902 Front St., Toledo; 419/691-6054; dinner for two ✖✖.*

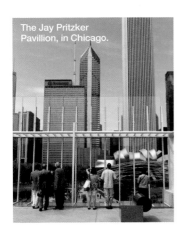

The Jay Pritzker Pavillion, in Chicago.

WHAT TO SEE + DO

ILLINOIS

Jay Pritzker Pavilion From Frank Gehry, an attention-getting civic monument and concert venue that serves as Chicago's public patio. *Millennium Park, Chicago; 312/742-1168; millenniumpark.org.*

McCormick Tribune Campus Center Iconoclastic Rem Koolhaas design, his first in the United States. *Illinois Institute of Technology, 3201 S. State St., Chicago; 312/567-3700; iit.edu.*

Modern Wing, Art Institute of Chicago Completed in 2009 by architect Renzo Piano, the 264,000-square-foot addition makes the institute the second largest art museum in the United States. *111 S. Michigan Ave., Chicago; 312/443-3600.*

IOWA

Des Moines Art Center Multi-wing building that over time brought three architectural greats together: Eliel Saarinen, I. M. Pei, and Richard Meier. *4700 Grand Ave., Des Moines; 515/277-4405; desmoinesartcenter.org.*

Des Moines Public Library Low building of glass and copper by architect David Chipperfield, with a "green" roof (the first in the city). *1000 Grand Ave., Des Moines; 515/283-4152; pldminfo.org.*

Merchants National Bank Designed by noted 20th-century architect Louis Sullivan, known as the "father of modernism." *833 Fourth Ave., Grinnell; 641/236-1626; grinnelliowa.gov.*

School of Art and Art History Partially cantilevered over an abandoned quarry, architect Steven Holl's structure feels like a box on stilts. Closed for renovation until 2011. *University of Iowa, 141 N. Riverside Dr., Iowa City; 319/335-1771; art.uiowa.edu.*

MINNESOTA

Guthrie Theater Designed by architect Jean Nouvel and home to one of America's top regional theater companies; the bar affords expansive views of the Mississippi. *818 S. Second St., Minneapolis; 612/377-2224; guthrietheater.org.*

Walker Art Center One of the country's most acclaimed cultural centers, with a striking 2005 addition by Herzog & de Meuron (perforated metal transforms a featureless box into a dazzling optical illusion). *1750 Hennepin Ave., Minneapolis; 612/375-7600; walkerart.org.*

OHIO

Campus Recreation Center Mesmerizing 350,000-square-foot maze of athletic facilities, dorms, classrooms, and a dining hall. *University of Cincinnati, 2820 Bearcat Way, Cincinnati; 513/556-5706; uc.edu.*

Contemporary Arts Center Architect Zaha Hadid's concrete-and-glass structure is made up of irregular doorways, stairways, and columns and radiates kinetic energy on a downtown corner. *44 E. Sixth St., Cincinnati; 513/345-8400; contemporaryarts center.org.*

Glass Pavilion, Toledo Museum of Art Designed by Japanese firm SANAA, an elegant, deceptively simple building showcasing the museum's glass collection. *2445 Monroe St.; 419/255-8000; toledomuseum.org.*

WISCONSIN

Milwaukee Art Museum Set on the shores of Lake Michigan, this cultural institution achieved iconic design status thanks to architect Santiago Calatrava's Quadracci Pavilion, which evokes tall ships soaring over a sea of space. *700 N. Art Museum Dr.; 414/224-3200; mam.org.*

A sundae from Whitey's Ice Cream, in Iowa City.

WHERE TO STAY NEXT

On the horizon: two design-forward hotels slated to debut in the next few years.

CINCINNATI, OHIO Adding new energy to the city's downtown revitalization: plans for the 2012 opening of a **21c Museum Hotel**, already a proven winner in Louisville, Kentucky (see page 78). After a $45 million renovation, the former Metropole Hotel will have approximately 160 guest rooms and a contemporary art museum with 8,000 square feet of exhibition space, all within walking distance of Cincinnati's Contemporary Arts Center and the Aronoff Center for the Arts.

MASON CITY, IOWA After decades of decline that led to an eventual closure, the **Historic Park Inn Hotel**—the world's last remaining Frank Lloyd Wright–designed hotel—is currently undergoing an $18 million renovation. The striking brick-and-terra-cotta structure, designed in the Prairie School style and completed in 1910, is being reimagined as a 28-suite boutique hotel and is scheduled to reopen in 2011.

STOP FOR SCOOPS

Dietsch Brothers Inc. Classic ice cream flavors and sherbet made in-house. *400 W. Main Cross St., Findlay, Ohio; 419/422-4474; dietschs.com.*

Kopp's Frozen Custard Local landmark famous for its indulgent custard and enormous burgers. *7631 W. Layton Ave., Greenfield, Wis.; 414/282-4312; kopps.com.*

Whitey's Ice Cream Pitch-perfect shakes, banana splits, and sundaes scooped by a cheerful teenage staff. *112 E. Washington St., Iowa City; 319/354-1200; whiteysicecream.com.*

KEY TO THE DINING PRICE ICONS   **X** UNDER $25   **XX** $25–$74   **XXX** $75–$149   **XXXX** $150–$299   **XXXXX** $300 AND UP

Photographed by Thomas Loof

THE NEW LOOK OF LAS VEGAS

WITH THE OPENING OF CITYCENTER, SERIOUS ARCHITECTURE AND DESIGN—AND A BIT OF AUTHENTIC URBAN TEXTURE—ARE STAKING A CLAIM AMID THE NEON-LIT RAZZLE-DAZZLE OF THE STRIP. BY KARRIE JACOBS

EACH MORNING, AS CLEANING CREWS SCRUB the traces of the nightly moving party from the sidewalks and the last revelers stare in wonderment at fresh-faced joggers, most of the Strip's casinos and hotels are revealed to be a bit less phantasmagorical and a bit more beige than they appeared the night before. But not CityCenter. The humongous $8.5 billion, 18-million-square-foot development that opened in December 2009 is the rare sort of Vegas spectacle that actually looks great—maybe even better—in the daytime. The jagged steel-and-glass peaks of architect Daniel Libeskind's luxury shopping mall, Crystals, glisten in the sunshine. The splashes of mustard yellow pop on the rakishly angled Veer condo towers by Chicago-based architect Helmut Jahn. Light plays off the glass exteriors of each of the major hotels—the 4,400-room Aria Resort & Casino, the 1,495-room Vdara Hotel & Spa, and the 392-room Mandarin Oriental—in a different way. The product of five years of feverish design and construction by casino developer and operator MGM Mirage (in partnership with a subsidiary of Dubai World) and a dramatic rescue last April from near bankruptcy, CityCenter is a study in nuance—a novelty in a town that does not exactly

trade in subtlety. It is also a bold statement of grown-up style and real architecture in a town not known for either.

Indeed, most of what we now associate with Las Vegas is more suburban than urban in form: huge, boxy buildings or Y-shaped towers strung along the Strip, tricked out to look like postcard versions of Paris or ancient Egypt. In the landmark 1972 book *Learning from Las Vegas,* architects Robert Venturi, Denise Scott Brown, and Steven Izenour famously described the local style as "the decorated shed." What this means is that most of the buildings in Las Vegas, no matter how ornate, are always formulated to contain as many square feet of gaming as possible and to maximize the views from the largest possible number of hotel rooms. Drive along the backside of the Strip, however, and all the illusion disappears: what you mostly see are naked concrete walls, like the side view of a Walmart.

Nonetheless, Las Vegas has become more urban in feel over the years, almost in spite of itself. Back in the 1960's and 1970's, explains Bobby Baldwin, CityCenter president and CEO and champion poker player, Las Vegas visitors were a sedentary bunch, checking in at one hotel/casino and staying

OPPOSITE: A night view of CityCenter, with the Daniel Libeskind–designed Crystals shopping center in the foreground.

CITYCENTER IS A BOLD STATEMENT OF GROWN-UP STYLE AND REAL ARCHITECTURE IN A TOWN NOT KNOWN FOR EITHER

put. "My parents were customers of Las Vegas, and they never left the Desert Inn, for example," Baldwin says. But in the 1990's, a building boom packed the Strip with a new generation of theme-park style properties, including Luxor, the Venetian, Bellagio, and New York New York, and the behavior of visitors changed. "As the Strip filled up more and more, there became less of a need to get into a car to go from one building to another, and people started walking," says Sven Van Assche, the garrulous vice president of design for MGM and the man who assembled the project's A-list architect lineup. Walking is now on par with gambling and drinking as a key Las Vegas pastime, and the Strip, thick with peripatetic tourists, is like a cross between Times Square and Bourbon Street.

The Las Vegas formula typically involves importing cultural artifacts that have been successful elsewhere: Celine Dion, Cirque du Soleil, or Jean-Georges Vongerichten. Until CityCenter opened, this was also the Las Vegas approach to urban design. Ancient Luxor, Paris, Venice, New York: the Strip is overstocked with imitations of other cities. CityCenter, by contrast, is the first city-themed development here that is not a copy. "We're not designing illusionist architecture anymore, where you have a box and you paint a blue ceiling on it," Libeskind says. Van Assche points to Bellagio (also an MGM property) as the dawn of a less literal brand of theming, meaning they borrowed "northern Italian vernacular" without appropriating an existing city. He sees CityCenter as a logical next step: "We decided that we're going to create something that's urban, something that's all about mixed use and the energy of great cities and place-making."

Unlike almost everything else in Las Vegas (with the exception of Steve Wynn's most recent towers), the buildings of CityCenter are emphatically three-dimensional. They don't go blank on the back side and, amazingly, they even look good from above. CityCenter is a complex puzzle of interlocking pieces, a whole menu of shapes, sizes, and materials—much like a real city—connected by a sinuous series of walkways and roads and bisected by a new tramline. And unlike major new developments in Dubai or Shanghai, the pedestrian experience here has been well thought through by professionals like the urban planners at Ehrenkrantz, Eckstut & Kuhn Architects, known for their seminal work on New York's Battery Park City, and the sophisticated landscape designers at Field Operations, famous for their collaboration on New York's High Line park. Van Assche believes the development's meandering pathways, routinely punctuated by sculptures such as Claes Oldenburg and Coosje van Bruggen's *Typewriter Eraser, Scale X* or Nancy Rubins's startling assemblage of canoes and rowboats, *Big Edge,* tend to humanize the

Outside the Julian Serrano restaurant at Aria Resort & Casino, below. OPPOSITE, CLOCKWISE FROM TOP LEFT: The bar on the 23rd floor of the Mandarin Oriental hotel; *Typewriter Eraser, Scale X* by Claes Oldenburg and Coosje van Bruggen, outside the hotel; a booth at Silk Road restaurant, in the Vdara Hotel; the exterior of Aria, designed by Cesar Pelli.

architecture. "We didn't want to create the monumentality that modern architecture is known for," Van Assche says. Indeed, designer David Rockwell, who collaborated with Libeskind on Crystals—they filled the mall with unique "landmarks," such as a three-story abstract

"WE DECIDED TO CREATE SOMETHING URBAN, ALL ABOUT MIXED-USE AND THE ENERGY OF GREAT CITIES" —ARCHITECT DANIEL LIBESKIND

structure called the Tree House—regards the meandering pathways as the exact thing that distinguishes CityCenter from the rest of Las Vegas. The plan offers an unusual degree of freedom in a town known for its "tightly controlled sight lines and flow of people," he says.

Of course, it's still Vegas: one low-rise corrugated metal building, so oddly shaped that it could be a Frank Gehry, turns out to be the Aria's theater, home to the Cirque du Soleil show *Viva Elvis*. And all this outward sophistication doesn't mean that the various CityCenter buildings aren't jam-packed with eye candy. At the Mandarin Oriental, for example, interior designer Adam Tihany tries to re-create the experience of contemporary Hong Kong. When guests step off the elevator at the 23rd-floor lobby, they encounter what he calls a "gold bullion wall," a shimmering blast of gilded geometry. "It's about power," Tihany says. The Aria has some 20 highly stylized restaurants and lounges: a brightly tiled tapas bar run by Bellagio restaurateur Julian Serrano looks as if it were airlifted in from Barcelona; Sage, a first Las Vegas venue for Chicago chef Shawn McClain, is the Midwest as reimagined by Parisian interior designer Jacques Garcia, with dark wood floors and Lalique lamps; Blossom, a Chinese restaurant designed by the New York firm Studio A, is decorated in gray concrete with inlaid mirrors forming an exquisite leaf pattern.

OPPOSITE: The courtyard of the Jean-Georges Steakhouse, at Aria.

Yes, there is nonstop interior design—and more art by the likes of Maya Lin and Frank Stella—but what truly distinguishes almost every building within the complex is the healthy relationship, unusual for Las Vegas, between indoors and outdoors. At the Vdara hotel, designed by Rafael Viñoly, there is a ground-floor restaurant called Silk Road, a new venue for chef Martin Heierling, who is known for his imaginative Pan-Asian cuisine. The interior, designed by Karim Rashid in florid gold and pink, has a biomorphic pink settee breaking through the glass exterior wall, literally bridging inside and out. Libeskind's Crystals, all swoopy inside like Eero Saarinen's landmark TWA terminal, has skylights throughout, allowing visitors to spot the surrounding buildings and actually judge the time of day. (The enlightened relationship between inside and out goes deeper: Aria, Vdara, Crystals, Mandarin Oriental, and Veer Towers have achieved LEED Gold certification, acknowledgment of the complex's energy- and resource-conserving features.)

Had it not been for the recent financial meltdown, CityCenter would have been the leading edge of a larger trend toward a more cosmopolitan Strip. Other slated developments, including the $4.8 billion Echelon, featuring modern architecture and branches of the chic Mondrian and Delano hotels, have run out of money and stopped construction. Baldwin contends that launching a major development in hard times, when everyone says the Strip can't absorb any more hotel rooms, never mind the condos, is more or less a Las Vegas tradition. "I have seen this movie many times before," he says. "The fact that it's happening in the tail end of what some people call the Great Recession is really of no consequence." He may be overstating the case, but the impressive buildings themselves seem to validate Baldwin's poker-king bravado, and they look to attract a new and more urbane customer to the city. "It won't be long before CityCenter will be considered a permanent fixture in Las Vegas," he says, "as if it had been here forever."

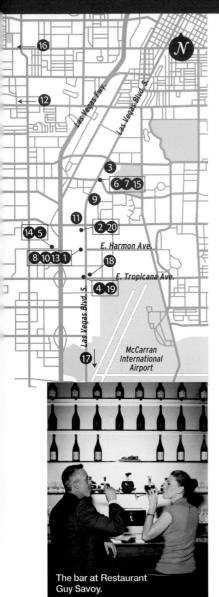

The bar at Restaurant Guy Savoy.

WHERE TO STAY

1. Aria Resort & Casino More than 4,000 guest rooms, 20 restaurants and lounges, and Cirque du Soleil's latest gravity-defying triumph, *Viva Elvis. 3730 Las Vegas Blvd. S.; 866/359-7757 or 702/590-7757; arialasvegas. com; doubles from $.*

2. Bellagio Palatial property turned bona fide icon (thanks in no small part to its dancing fountains). *3600 Las Vegas Blvd. S.; 888/987-6667 or 702/693-7111; bellagio.com; doubles from $.*

3. Encore Las Vegas Gardens, pools, and a light-filled casino make Steve Wynn's latest hotel a new kind of desert oasis. *3121 Las Vegas Blvd. S.; 888/320-7125 or 702/770-7171; encorelasvegas. com; suites from $.*

4. Mandarin Oriental Evoking contemporary Hong Kong in the heart of CityCenter. *3752 Las Vegas Blvd. S.; 800/526-6566 or 702/590-8888; mandarinoriental. com/lasvegas; doubles from $.*

5. Vdara Hotel & Spa Exclusive all-suite property with an 18,000-square-foot spa—and no casino. *2600 W. Harmon Ave.; 866/745-7767 or 702/590-2767; vdara.com; suites from $.*

6. Wynn Las Vegas Sequestered from the Strip by gardens and waterfalls, this game-changing hotel quickly became the epitome of Vegas luxury. *3131 Las Vegas Blvd. S.; 877/321-9966 or 702/770-7000; wynnlasvegas.com; doubles from $.*

WHERE TO EAT

7. Alex Robust French Riviera cuisine in a space as majestic as a vintage ocean liner. *Wynn Las Vegas, 3131 Las Vegas Blvd. S.; 702/248-3463; prix fixe menu* ✗✗✗ *per person.*

8. Blossom Authentic Chinese cuisine in an exquisite setting of concrete, mirrors, and wooden latticework, designed by New York firm Studio A. *Aria Resort & Casino, 3730 Las Vegas Blvd. S.; 877/ 230-2742; dinner for two* ✗✗✗.

9. David Burke Las Vegas Interiors as over-the-top as they come, matched by decadent dishes (lobster cocktail infused with chili butter). *The Venetian, 3355 Las Vegas Blvd. S.; 702/ 414-7111; dinner for two* ✗✗✗.

10. Julian Serrano Funky tapas bar channeling the ambience of Barcelona. *Aria Resort & Casino, 3730 Las Vegas Blvd. S.; 877/ 230-2742; dinner for two* ✗✗✗.

11. Restaurant Guy Savoy Dining as a marquee event, replete with bread sommeliers, jewel-like oyster platters, and an incomparable cheese cart. *Caesars Palace, 3570 Las Vegas Blvd. S.; 877/346-4642; dinner for two* ✗✗✗.

12. Rosemary's Restaurant Vegas chefs flock to this convivial joint on Sundays. *8125 W. Sahara Ave.; 702/869-2251; prix fixe menu* ✗✗ *per person.*

13. Sage Seafood standout from chef Shawn McClain. *Aria Resort & Casino, 3730 Las Vegas Blvd. S.; 877/230-2742; dinner for two* ✗✗✗.

14. Silk Road Mediterranean fare served against a vibrantly colored backdrop. *Vdara Hotel & Spa, 2600 W. Harmon Ave.; 866/745-7767; lunch for two* ✗✗.

15. SW Steakhouse For wet-aged Nebraska beef steaks. *Wynn Las Vegas, 3131 Las Vegas Blvd. S.; 702/770-3325; dinner for two* ✗✗✗.

16. Vintner Grill An all-white interior and dishes from every corner of the Mediterranean. *10100 W. Charleston Blvd., suite 150, Summerlin; 702/214-5590; dinner for two* ✗✗✗.

The atrium at the Wynn Las Vegas.

KEY TO THE HOTEL PRICE ICONS $ UNDER $250 $$ $250–$499 $$$ $500–$749 $$$$ $750–$999 $$$$$ $1,000 AND UP

KEY TO THE DINING PRICE ICONS ✗ UNDER $25   ✗✗ $25–$74   ✗✗✗ $75–$149   ✗✗✗✗ $150–$299   ✗✗✗✗✗ $300 AND UP

Aria Resort
& Casino.

Top Las Vegas Cocktail Bars
J. C. Reed, Bellagio's director of concierge services, picks four of his favorite spots.

17. Blue Martini "Known as the best happy hour in town, with four different bars and forty specialty martinis. My pick: the pomegranate." *Town Square, 6593 Las Vegas Blvd. S.; 702/949-2583; drinks for two ✕✕.*

18. Centrifuge "A fun place to get the party started, especially since it's just steps away from thc nightclub Ctudio 54." *MGM Grand, 3799 Las Vegas Blvd. S.; 702/891-1111; drinks for two ✕✕.*

19. Mandarin Bar "On the twenty-third floor overlooking the Vegas skyline, it's a respite from the bustling bars on the Strip. A team of molecular mixologists is on hand to develop customized concoctions on request. There's also a VIP room available by reservation." *Mandarin Oriental, 3752 Las Vegas Blvd. S.; 888/881-9367; drinks for two ✕✕.*

20. Yellowtail Japanese Restaurant and Lounge "Sit at the bar and order the following two items: a kiwi crush cocktail and the popping spicy crab roll. Yes, Pop Rocks in a sushi roll—your mouth has never had anything like it." *Bellagio, 3600 Las Vegas Blvd. S.; 702/693-7223; drinks for two ✕✕.*

Photographed by Buff Strickland

ART OASIS

IN THE VAST TEXAS DESERT, AN UNLIKELY CULTURAL MECCA SHOWCASES A
GROUNDBREAKING COLLECTION OF CONTEMPORARY WORKS. BY PAUL ALEXANDER

FROM A CHAIR NEAR THE FRONT WINDOW OF THE MARFA BOOK COMPANY,

the center of civic and social activity in this speck of a town (population 2,400) in far west Texas, Lynn Goode says, "You sit here and the whole world comes to you." It's a seemingly incongruous statement. But because Marfa—which is located some 180 miles southeast of El Paso and 57 miles north of the Mexican border—has become one of the hippest art communities in the country, almost anyone might wander through the front door. "Tommy Lee Jones has a ranch nearby," says Goode, the bookstore's former owner. "One day, Ian Schrager came in and bought *Hip Hotels*, a book that includes his properties, from the manager! Then there was the time Julia Roberts came in and bought a CD. *People* magazine called to find out what CD she bought. So I said, 'I'm not sure. I think it was something by Lyle Lovett.' I thought I was being funny, but the reporter didn't get the joke."

Goode and her then-husband, Tim Crowley, a successful Houston-based attorney, were the driving force behind the "new" Marfa. "In 1997, we passed through on the way to somewhere else," she says. Not an easy thing to do, since Marfa is in the middle of nowhere: to be exact, on a highland plain in an upper corner of the vast Chihuahuan Desert. To get to Marfa, you have to fly to either El Paso or Midland, rent a car, and drive for three hours (unless you have a private jet and fly into Marfa's minuscule municipal airport). "We were driving back to Houston," Goode explains, "and we stopped in Marfa. It was four o'clock in the morning—and as we stood in front of this old, abandoned grain warehouse I knew we needed to buy that building and come here."

Goode and Crowley did buy the building, which they renovated and converted into a theater—one of the best performance spaces for miles. Over the next several years they also bought and renovated about 24 commercial buildings and homes, among them the former hotel that became the bookstore. They were not alone: in recent years, area businessman Joe Duncan purchased and restored the landmark Hotel Paisano, and Austin hotelier Liz Lambert, whose family has ties to west Texas, acquired the dilapidated Thunderbird and Capri motels. The 24-room Thunderbird, which reopened in early 2005, juxtaposes contemporary design with Western touches (handcrafted furniture in pecan wood; cowhides on polished concrete floors); across the street, the Capri now serves as space for music events, parties, and photo shoots. Lambert's latest project, El Cosmico, consists of lodgings in restored vintage trailers, eco-friendly yurts, and tepees on a site just outside town.

Marfa has also been overrun by art galleries. Drive through town and you see them everywhere: the Eugene Binder Gallery, Galleri Urbane, Marfa Studio of Arts, and Ballroom Marfa. The opening of Ballroom, an art space founded by Fairfax Dorn and Virginia Lebermann, was the social event of the season. "We have a love for west Texas and the landscape," Dorn says. "We were visiting Marfa and felt there needed to be a place where you could combine art, music, and film. That's what Ballroom Marfa does—it breaks down boundaries."

JUST WHY MARFA HAS BECOME AN ART MECCA can be summed up in a single name: Donald Judd. One of the most important minimalist artists to

OPPOSITE: The Block, Donald Judd's former residence. PREVIOUS SPREAD, FROM LEFT: Judd's 15 untitled concrete works (1980–84); spartan quarters at the Thunderbird Motel.

TOP, FROM LEFT: The Marfa Book Company; a room in Donald Judd's former residence; a billboard on the outskirts of town. BELOW: Judd's 100 aluminum boxes (1982–86), on display at the Chinati Foundation.

JUST WHY MARFA HAS BECOME AN ART MECCA CAN BE SUMMED UP IN A SINGLE NAME: DONALD JUDD

come out of the New York art world in the 1960's, Judd, having grown tired of living and working in the confines of the city, moved to Marfa in 1973. (He had been to Van Horn, 74 miles north of Marfa, in 1946 as a serviceman on his way from Alabama to Los Angeles en route to Korea; years later, in 1971, he had passed through Marfa.) In the late seventies, with the financial support of the Dia Art Foundation, an organization funded by Schlumberger heiress Philippa de Menil, Judd began buying up property in and around town—principally a 340-acre former army base called Fort D.A. Russell. Judd renamed the base the Art Museum of the Pecos and set out to establish permanent facilities to display his own work, along with pieces by fellow sculptor John Chamberlain and fluorescent-light works by Dan Flavin.

In the town itself, Judd, with Dia, bought the vacant 24,000-square-foot Wool & Mohair building. Renovations were overseen by Judd, and 23 of Chamberlain's car-wreck sculptures, dating from 1972 to 1983, were permanently installed. The Dia-Judd partnership ended in 1986 after a falling-out that was resolved—only when Judd threatened legal action—by Dia transferring the ownership of all its property and art in Marfa over to Judd. Judd then changed the institution's name to the Chinati Foundation, for the nearby mountain.

Judd bought a separate house in Marfa for his own living space, fenced it off, and called it the Block. In the late 1980's, as the sales and value of his artworks boomed, he began to buy up more

and more of the town—the old Marfa National Bank, a supermarket, a grocery store. Ultimately, he owned nine buildings in Marfa, as well as 34,000 acres and three houses outside of town. After Judd's death in 1994, oversight of the Chinati Foundation was assumed by Marianne Stockebrand, his companion during the last five years of his life, and Rob Weiner, his art assistant.

In time, Chinati's collection would feature an outdoor sculpture by Claes Oldenburg and Coosje van Bruggen; works by Roni Horn and Ilya Kabakov; a multipart installation, occupying six U-shaped former army barracks, of colored fluorescent-light sculptures by Flavin named *Untitled (Marfa Project),* the artist's final work;

Dan Flavin's *Untitled (Marfa Project)* (1996), below.

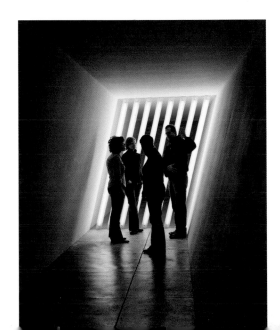

and Judd's masterpiece—100 shimmering boxes, 41 by 51 by 72 inches, made of mill aluminum and displayed in two former artillery sheds, cavernous buildings that have had their doors replaced with huge glass windows to let the sun spill in. A companion work by Judd featuring 15 concrete boxlike forms is displayed outside the artillery sheds in a field.

Because of Judd, Flavin, and others, Marfa today is a pilgrimage site on the international art landscape. When it was founded, in 1883, its only relation to high culture was its name. A railroad engineer's wife who read Russian novels (in Russian) baptized the town with the name of a minor character in *The Brothers Karamazov*. "At first, Marfa was a watering stop on the railroad," says Cecilia Thompson, a local historian. "But it soon became a cattleman's town, with the huge herds that came west in the decades following the Civil War." Marfa was still very much a rancher's outpost in 1930, when the Hotel Paisano, its most famous building, opened its doors. Designed by noted Southwest architect Henry Trost, who studied with Frank Lloyd Wright, the Spanish colonial–Revival structure was based on Trost's design for the Val Verde Hotel, in Socorro, New Mexico, and marked by "red tile roof parapets, delicate ironwork balconies, and areas of plasteresque ornament," as described in a published account of the hotel.

The high point of the Paisano's history came in 1955, when the cast and crew of *Giant* occupied the hotel during the film's three-month shoot in and around Marfa. "It was the most exciting thing we've had in Marfa," says Lucy Garcia, a town native who was one of the teenagers to hang out at the hotel during the shoot. "Rock Hudson and Elizabeth Taylor were here, but they were a little too big for Marfa. They gave us autographs but wouldn't allow any pictures. James Dean let us take pictures of him at the hotel and showed us the lasso rope trick he was learning for the movie. He told jokes. He had such a pretty giggle."

A drought in the 1950's coincided with a collapse of the cattle industry and weakened the town's economy. Consequently, Judd was able to buy a lot of property in the community in the 80's. But he didn't do much with the buildings when he bought them. "Judd wanted to put his art in the natural landscape. He did little, if anything, to the town as he bought it up," Thompson says. "Judd never mingled. He actually didn't make an impact on the town—its façade, that is. That wouldn't happen until Judd died and civic leaders like Goode and Crowley moved in. They invested in the town. Take Main Street, for example. They're responsible for waking it up." Part of that revitalization involves the Hotel Paisano. It fell into disrepair in the 80's and 90's. In 2001, Joe Duncan bought the building for back taxes ($185,000) and restored it to its original splendor. James Dean's room looks just as it did 55 years ago—and there are still no telephones in the rooms.

MARFA IS A PLACE FULL OF TRADITIONS. JUDD himself inaugurated one of them in 1987: the annual Open House during Columbus Day weekend. The town plays host to a party that includes art exhibits, readings, a street dance, and, in 2009, a concert by the electronic musician Dan Deacon. Though Open House almost doubles the town's population, all events are free.

But the tradition that has come to define the city most is not even explainable. Every Labor Day weekend, a festival celebrates the Marfa Mystery Lights. Just outside town, at a certain bend in Route 90, you can stand on the side of the road in the desert and, looking south toward Mexico, see fleeting visions of light that flash about in the sky. First recorded in 1881 by a young cowboy named Robert P. Ellison, who was tending a herd of cattle and thought he had spotted the campfires of Apache Indians, the lights—still unaccounted for by science—appear and disappear, and seem to divide and travel in the night sky. Near the viewing site where you can best see the Marfa Mystery Lights, a plaque explains why they cannot be physically located: The flickering lights are "an unusual phenomenon similar to a miracle where atmospheric conditions produced by the interaction of cold and warm layers of air blend together so it can be seen from afar but not up close. The mystery of the lights will remain unsolved."

OPPOSITE: Marfa's iconic water tower.

Outside the Marfa Book Company.

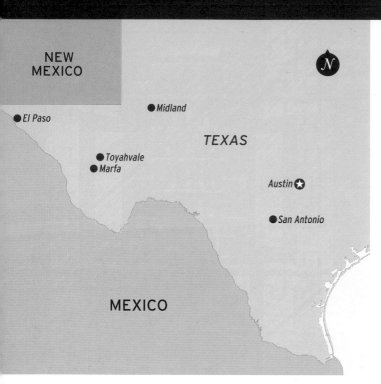

NEW MEXICO

El Paso

Midland

TEXAS

Toyahvale
Marfa

Austin ★

San Antonio

MEXICO

Thunderbird Hotel Locally run since 1959, with updates from Liz Lambert: Think Malin + Goetz amenities and a stocked vinyl library, with event space across the street. *601 W. San Antonio St.; 432/729-1984; thunderbirdmarfa. com; doubles from $.*

WHERE TO EAT

Jett's Grill Feast on classic Texan dishes like rib eye or pan-seared trout on the open-air patio. *Hotel Paisano, 207 N. Highland Ave.; 432/729-3838; dinner for two ✗✗.*

Maiya's Owned by a local artist with a sustainable mind-set. *103 N. Highland Ave.; 432/729-4410; dinner for two ✗✗.*

WHAT TO SEE + DO

Ballroom Marfa Cultural space that hosts music events, film screenings, and art exhibitions. *108 E. San Antonio St.; 432/729-3600; ballroommarfa.org.*

Balmorhea State Park Ancient springs where Apache Indians once watered their horses; now the site of a spring-fed swimming pool, adobe brick cabins, and bathhouse built during the New Deal. *59 miles north of Marfa in Toyahvale, Tex.; 432/375-2370; tpwd.state.tx.us.*

Chinati Foundation Artist Donald Judd made good use of this former military fort: it now holds some of the best large-scale modern art installations in the country. Visits to the museum are available by guided tour only, Wednesday through Sunday. *1 Cavalry Row; 432/729-4362; chinati.org.*

Crowley Theater One of the finest music venues in west Texas. *98 S. Austin St.; no phone.*

Marfa Book Company Half shop and half art gallery, with free Wi-Fi. *105 S. Highland Ave.; 432/729-3906; marfabookco.com.*

WHERE TO STAY

El Cosmico Hotelier Liz Lambert's latest gift to Marfa—a collection of revamped travel trailers, yurts, and a Sioux tepee on 18 desert acres (pottery studio and darkroom to come). *802 S. Highland Ave.; 877/822-1950 or 432/729-1950; elcosmico.com; trailers from $.*

Hotel Paisano Deco-era respite that hosted James Dean and Elizabeth Taylor during the filming of *Giant*. *207 N. Highland Ave.; 866/729-3669 or 432/729-3669; hotelpaisano.com; doubles from $.*

Downtown Marfa.

KEY TO THE HOTEL PRICE ICONS	$ UNDER $250	$$ $250–$499	$$$ $500–$749	$$$$ $750–$999	$$$$$ $1,000 AND UP
KEY TO THE DINING PRICE ICONS	✗ UNDER $25	✗✗ $25–$74	✗✗✗ $75–$149	✗✗✗✗ $150–$299	✗✗✗✗✗ $300 AND UP

Outside the
Crowley Theater.

Liz Lambert's Essential Marfa

The hotelier names her favorite spots in town.

RESTAURANTS

Cochineal "Global food by an ex-Manhattanite in an adobe-meets-modern building." *115 W. San Antonio St.; 432/729-3300; dinner for two* ✗✗.

Food Shark "Fantastic Mediterranean dishes served out of a crazy 1960's delivery truck, with an eight-track tape player broadcasting hits from yesteryear." *Under the pavilion between the railroad tracks and Marfa Book Company; 432/386-6540; lunch for two* ✗.

NIGHTLIFE

Padre's "Sit on the patio, play vintage pinball, or enjoy one of the many live bands that pass through town." *209 W. El Paso St.; 432/729-4425.*

SHOPPING

Farm Stand Marfa "The wide array of produce points to a thriving gardening culture that few expect in the high plains desert." Held on Saturdays. *Under the pavilion between the railroad tracks and Marfa Book Company; no phone.*

JM Dry Goods "Owner Michelle Teague moved here from Brooklyn after falling for the town while working on *There Will Be Blood.* Her shop sells vintage clothing, accessories, and home items." *107 S. Dean St.; 917/548-7606.*

CONTRIBUTORS

CONTRIBUTORS

PAUL ALEXANDER is the author of eight books and two plays. He has written about politics for *Rolling Stone*.

RAUL BARRENECHE, the author of seven books, including *Pacific Modern* (Rizzoli), has written about architecture for *Elle Decor*, *Interior Design*, and the *New York Times*.

GABRIELLA DE FERRARI, a writer and art historian in New York City, is a contributing editor for *Travel + Leisure*.

CHARLES GANDEE, a former editor at *Vogue*, contributed to the monograph *Thad Hayes: The Tailored Interior* (Rizzoli).

KARRIE JACOBS, the founding editor-in-chief of *Dwell* and a faculty member of New York City's School of Visual Arts, is a contributing editor for *Travel + Leisure*.

MATT LEE AND TED LEE are *Travel + Leisure* contributing editors and authors of *The Lee Bros. Simple, Fresh, Southern* (Clarkson Potter).

PETER JON LINDBERG, whose *Travel + Leisure* essays "In Defense of Tourism," "Unhappy to Serve You," and "Stop the Music!" earned him a 2010 ASME nomination, is the magazine's editor-at-large.

M. G. LORD teaches writing and literature at the University of Southern California, is a frequent contributor to the *New York Times*, and is the author of the family memoir *Astro Turf* (Walker & Company).

JULIAN RUBINSTEIN is the executive producer of One Day Film Project and is currently at work on his second book.

BRUCE SCHOENFELD, the wine and spirits editor of *Travel + Leisure*, is the author of *The Match* (HarperCollins) and has written for *Saveur, Wine Spectator,* and *Sports Illustrated*.

MARIA SHOLLENBARGER is the deputy editor of the *Financial Times'* magazine *How to Spend It*.

GARY SHTEYNGART, the author of *Super Sad True Love Story* (Random House), teaches writing at Columbia University.

OLIVER STRAND, a New York City–based food writer, is at work on a book about hunting with Martin Picard, the chef of Au Pied de Cochon, in Montreal.

JEFF WISE is a *Travel + Leisure* contributing editor and the author of *Extreme Fear: The Science of Your Mind in Danger* (Palgrave MacMillan).

PHOTOGRAPHERS

Ball & Albanese
Martha Camarillo
Brown W Cannon III
João Canziani
David Cicconi
Lisa Eisner
Blasius Erlinger
Andrea Fazzari
Thayer Allyson Gowdy
Thomas Loof
Kevin Miyazaki
Marcus Nilson
Annie Schlechter
Jessica Schwartzberg
Hugh Stewart
Buff Strickland